REV. JAMES R. HAWK

Heavenly
MORNING
Glories

WESTBOW
PRESS®
A DIVISION OF THOMAS NELSON
& ZONDERVAN

WestBow Press books may be ordered through booksellers or by contacting:

WestBow Press
A Division of Thomas Nelson & Zondervan
1663 Liberty Drive
Bloomington, IN 47403
www.westbowpress.com
1 (866) 928-1240

ISBN: 978-1-9736-3228-3 (sc)
ISBN: 978-1-9736-3227-6 (hc)
ISBN: 978-1-9736-3229-0 (e)

Library of Congress Control Number: 2018907609

Print information available on the last page.

WestBow Press rev. date: 07/16/2018

TO OUR SONS

Meditations

The Banqueting House

He brought me to the banqueting house and his banner over me was love (Song of Solomon 2:4).

Does this verse tell of the future gathering of Christ and his Church? This view seems to harmonize with other Scriptures of the Bible to that end.

When Jesus fellowshipped with his disciples at his last supper he stated (in all three Synoptic Gospels) these words:

> I will not drink henceforth of this fruit of the vine until the day when I drink it new with you in my Father's kingdom.

In the Hebrew language the banqueting house means house of wine.

In Revelation 19 a yet future supper is described between Jesus and his Church. This supper seems to have included at least the following:

- A time of honoring Jesus
- A time of gladness and rejoicing
- A time when the Church will literally, or symbolically, be dressed in white, representing righteousness

- A time when the Church will have been made ready for the occasion
- A time when certain people are said to be blessed to be called to the marriage supper
- A time when Jesus will uniquely present the bride (Church) to himself, implied from Ephesians 5:27,

> That he might present to himself a glorious church,
> not having spot or wrinkle, or any such thing; but
> that it should be holy and without blemish

If the wine house of Song of Solomon 2:4 is the place of the wedding supper of Revelation 19, then additional insights to our Heavenly future may be gleaned from this Old Testament book.

These insights result from the generally accepted view that the Book, Song of Solomon, consists of back and forth role playing between the Church, represented by a Shulamite woman, and Christ, portrayed by Solomon.

An immediate insight is that deep contrition over sin as a prerequisite to entering the banqueting house/wedding supper. Chapter 1, verse 4, infers contrition:

> I am black.

This confession is followed by suggested interruption from Solomon, i.e., Christ:

> But comely (loveable).

Our thoughts are carried to Romans 5:8:

Another insight into our being gathered to the banqueting house/wedding supper is that we must first be individually drawn to the conviction that we are sinners. The Shulamite woman responds,

Draw me, we will run after thee.

How interesting are the me and we__ that we are drawn singularly into a plural body, representing the Church!

Jesus stated, in the Gospel of John 6:42, the necessity of being drawn:

> No man can come to me, except the father which sent
> me draw him: and I will raise him up in the last day

There are additional insights which are implied in the verse:

> He brought me to the banqueting house and his
> banner over me was love.

If Christ brings us to the banqueting house/wedding supper, then the implication seems true that we could not find the way of our own doing. Such is the power of his salvation.

The Scriptures of the banqueting house allude to a personal salvation, i.e. "he brought me..." Also, there seems to be something of our royalty, which identifies with our peculiar position (1 Peter 2:9).

Perhaps the greatest insight from Song of Solomon 2:4 is the confession that every Christian is conquered by the love of Christ____ his love demonstrated for all at Calvary.

We leave the meditation surrounding the banqueting house with reflection that the Book, Song of Solomon, is not totally clear in every verse. We might easily grasp those verses of apparent simplicity but hesitate where deep intimacy is implied.

It is suggested that our limited understanding of the Song of Solomon may be due to the shortcomings of an earthy language, incapable of describing Heavenly things.

Morning Glories No. 1

It is of the Lord's mercies that we are not consumed, because his compassions fail not. They are new every morning: great is thy faithfulness (Lamentations 3:22-23).

How wonderful, that God's love for you is new each morning! You are now camped beside a great Heavenly blessing, like daily manna in the wilderness__ which we call a morning glory.

It is impossible to take in the depth of God's love, realizing that, on our best day, we woefully need a savior.

That God's love is new each morning tells you about your yesterdays. They are behind. You can have a new beginning. Forgiveness is available by confessing your sins, which are washed away by Christ's atoning blood at Calvary (Revelation 1:5). Can there be any word from Heaven why your Lord is so passionate with you each day? The most heart-stirring answer may be hinted from the words of Jesus "that where I am there ye may be also" (John 14:3). Each day that you are not at your Heavenly home, you are missed.

The ever-newness of God's love contrasts to our love for one another, which is often taken-for-granted.

This lamentation refutes any suggestion that God is a bully god, a consuming fire, devoid of any mercy. He does not carry grudges, does not delight in our afflictions. He is the perfection of a father. His love is new__ every morning. Hallelujah!

> So thou, O son of man, I have set thee a watchman into the house of Israel; therefore thou shalt hear the word at my mouth and warn them from me (Ezekiel 33:7).

> Say unto them, As I live, saith the Lord God, I have no pleasure in the death of the wicked (Ezekiel 33:11);

> Come now, and let us reason together, saith the Lord: though your sins be as scarlet, they shall be as white as snow; though they be red like crimson, they shall be as wool (Isaiah 1:18).

Morning Glories No. 2

Weeping may endure for a night, but joy cometh in
the morning (Psalms 30:5).

Rarely do anxieties and burdens last for only one night. More
than likely there are long nights of many days, weeks, and
possibly years of anguish. However, sufferings have a stopping point.
Sometimes peace and tranquility come suddenly___ like the quiet
after a violent storm. We call this newfound peace and tranquility
"joy in the morning."

Some problems are resolvable in only one day__ allowing "joy
in the morning." A common problem is that of strained relationships
with others___ and too much pride to acknowledge a personal
mistake or misunderstanding. Early marital disagreements are
common one-day problems that may stretch out into days and weeks.

Recalling my own experiences, I called those strained marital
episodes the "three-day spats." They occurred over fifty years ago.
But I still recall the symptoms during our first year of marriage.
Neither I nor my wife wanted to admit any wrong. Consequently,
many inconveniences occurred. Soiled laundry piled up. Over-
cooked eggs and burned toast were ungently laid on the breakfast
table. No goodnight kisses were shared. Sometimes the house- pet

laid low. Faces were turned toward the wall if sleeping together occurred. An apology for nearly anything would have been accepted after about three days. We had too much stubborn pride in those days. Now, some fifty years later, we look back and laugh.

God's word provides additional insights for discovering peace and tranquility, or joy in the morning. I especially like Psalms 126:5-6.

> They that sow in tears shall reap in joy. He that goeth forth and weepeth, bearing precious seed, shall doubtless come again with rejoicing, bringing his sheaves with him.

The above verse gives additional direction. Instead of constant tears we can sow precious seed by being active, and thereby get our minds off ourselves.

God has infinite ways to change stormy nights of personal sorrow into "joy in the morning." Some of God's ways may seem a bit harsh. I recall, for example, an incident in the Bible where children mocked the baldness of God's prophet___ and God destroyed the youth with bears. Seems to me like a good bear-licking would have been sufficient punishment.

Whether harsh or not, God's ways of changing burdensome nights to joyous mornings are not always in our circle of capabilities. Many burdens have passed well beyond simple apologies in strained relationships.

The following personal experience has saddened me at times and does not seem to me to be inspirational. The only reason which I have included it in this meditation is to more completely reveal God's ways in fulfilling Psalms 30:5.

THE SALVATION OF MARVIN BAIRD

In 1981 I officiated the funeral of Harvey Joyner in a church which I then pastored____ and used Psalms 30:5 during that service. A retired machinist in his seventies, Harvey had relocated from Michigan with his wife Rosie, had received Jesus as his Lord and Savior, and I had the privilege of baptizing him. Harvey subsequently died within a few months from his lingering cancer.

On Monday morning after the funeral a very large man approached me at church with food dishes which had been used in serving Harvey's family. He asked me to clarify the meaning of the meditation/funeral verse. In the simplest manner, I explained that God's children, like Harvey, may experience unusual suffering while on earth. But now, a new beginning had begun in Harvey's life, by his trust in Jesus Christ for forgiveness of sins____ and that he was enjoying an eternal morning of health with his Lord.

That morning I became acquainted with Marvin Baird

After only a few Sundays Marvin showed up for worship service. I had learned from Rosie that Marvin had attended to Harvey's bathroom needs during his lengthy illness. Within days Marvin professed faith in Jesus as his Lord and Savior, and I baptized the large man____ requiring the assistance of a layman. Marvin's weight may have approached 400 pounds.

My joy over Marvin's presence was soon troubled, upon learning that he was living under the same roof of a nearby divorced daughter of Harvey and Rosie. What would the church community think? I became distressed.

I soon learned that Marvin was a Vietnam Veteran, a homeless soul, wandering about in this world, helping the Joyner family. After his baptism, I overheard Marvin inform someone that he had to go to the local hospital to check on a large toe which had become blood red in color.

During the fall of 1981 I made countless visits to the hospital to visit Marvin. The toe had been amputated, followed shortly by removal of his left leg, below the knee.

During one hospital visit Marvin shrugged away his pain long enough to ask, "reverend, how can I know that I am truly saved? There are things which I haven't told you. I was a Green Berea in Vietnam, and my past is troubling".

I reminded Marvin of the great love and forgiveness of God, through Christ Jesus, which wrought eternal life. He seemed comforted, adding that he would help me in the church community when he got out of the hospital.

But that day I glanced at Marvin's remaining leg. Small and innumerable red spots contrasted with the white hospital sheet. I could only suppose that he had a blood circulation problem.

A few days later I visited Marvin, sitting in bed, both legs had been removed. Perspiring, the morphine was of little benefit in helping his pain.

Some say that he apparently died of a blood clot.

The few friends of Marvin in this life collected money for burial in the city cemetery. His gravestone simply reads,

MARVIN BAIRD__ A BIG MAN WITH A BIG HEART

The story of Marvin Baird may be one of extremes, where God allowed suffering and death to fulfill the truth of Psalms 30:5. From my perspective, the story is mixed with sadness and rejoicing. I now understand only some of Marvin's nighttime of suffering, but I would like to know more about his joy in the morning.

The Full Quiver

Who would consider comparing a Godly father to an archer, and likening his children to arrows in the quiver? The metaphor targets strong qualities of a righteous father.

NO FAVORITE ARROWS IN THE QUIVER

The archer does not contemplate which arrow to use, for they are of equal value.

Favoritism is as old as the human race. It seemed the right thing to do in many Old Testament families. Jacob's adoring of Joseph over his brethren seems flagrant. King David's favor for rebellious Absalom proved tragic.

That many fathers of the Old Testament had more than one wife may explain instances of open favoritism, but favoritism can never be approved.

The subtleties of favoritism abound in modern families. If you are a caring parent, you may be observed for innocent-like favoritism more than you realize. In the words of the poet, Robert Frost:

> O wad some power the giftie gie us to see oursels as
> others see us!

ARROWS ARE A REFLECTION OF THE ARCHER

Although there are no favorite arrows, there is a particular beauty of workmanship in each. There can be no "trusted" arrow, for then the quiver would contain only one. The archer has a story to tell that values each arrow

The Godly father will do well to see beauty and uniqueness in each of his children. If his grandchildren are the greatest in the world, then he should be prepared to reveal a positive story about each.

ARROWS MUST BE CAREFULLY MAINTAINED

If part of an arrow is damaged, then it will bring disappointment. Routine inspections are a must.

The issues of children's privacy versus their oversight must be dealt with early by caring parents. As a parent with authority, you may have an infrequent occasion to remind an obstinate teen that you hold the title to the home. I recall an incident some thirty years ago when I required our youngest son to write a paper on the subject "Why Dad is King of the Mountain." I'm saving the original for his young children.

ARROWS, WHEN RELEASED, HAVE DIRECTION

The archer does not aimlessly launch a prized arrow in any direction, ___ unless he is like the archer of 2 Kings who released an arrow towards the sun, and which downward flight found the heart of wicked, and disguised, King Ahab.

Godly fathers provide direction to their children by self-discipline, honest work, and patient mentoring.

GODLY HOMES HAVE GODLY PARENTS

The father-children relationships are only part of the family. The foundation of Godly relationships must spring from a Godly home.

> Except the Lord build the house, they labour in vain that build it: except the Lord keep the city, the watchman waketh but in vain (Psalms 127:1).

> Thy wife shall be as a fruitful vine by the sides of thine house; thy children like olive plants round about thy table (Psalms 128:3).

The Godly wife and mother is a fruit-bearer about her home. Her vine-like nature means that she clings to her family, adding fruit and beauty.

God's Provision For Prodigals

Luke 15 and Ruth 1:1-6

THE PRODIGAL SON AND THE PRODIGAL FAMILY

The New Testament relates the parable-story of the prodigal son, while the Book of Ruth describes the misadventures of a prodigal family. Both accounts have some similarities:

We know that the prodigal son was a freewheeling spender who carried off part of the family fortune into a far country, that he wasted his resources on sinful living, and that he ended up feeding swine. In time he realized how good it was back home, and then he returned that way.

The prodigal family was headed by Elimelech, with his wife Naomi, who left the home country of Bethlehem during hard times, journeying also into a far country called Moab. This family fell upon harder times in Moab. Elimelech died, as did the two sons (after marrying local women). And like the prodigal son, bitter Naomi turned her eyes back toward the home country.

Both the prodigal son and the prodigal family represented members of the family of God. They were not, in some salvation sense, "lost", but rather out-of-place. The out-of-place emphasis follows from examination of the two parables which precede that of the prodigal son: (1) the first parable describes one sheep out of a flock of 100 that went astray, i.e., belonging to the flock but temporarily out-of-place, and (2) the second parable tells of one silver coin from a collection of ten that was temporarily misplaced. Clearly, the emphasis is on people and objects out-of-place.

THE BEGINNINGS OF PRODIGALS

There is probably not a one-answer-fits-all, but the old saying "grass is greener on the other side" may be high on the list. This worn-out adage might fit many who become displaced, such as the following:

- Adam and Eve thought life would be better after eating the forbidden fruit.
- Lot must have thought life would be better in Sodom.
- Jonah might have thought life would be better while on the run.
- Abram took Sarah into Egypt, thinking life would be better.

GOD'S PROVISION FOR PRODIGALS

Because God so dearly loves us, he has provided grace for all who are out-of-place to return home.

> Come now, and let us reason together, saith the Lord: though your sins be as scarlet, they shall be as white as snow; thou they be red like crimson, they shall be as wool. (Isaiah 1:18)

THE PROVISION OF REALIZATION

The blessed Scriptures of Luke 15 teach that the prodigal son "came to himself." This is the work of God's grace on both the conscience and the mind that jolted the prodigal into reality.

Likewise, Naomi counted three graves in Moab, and came to the realization of her out-of-place condition.

Every Christian should periodically assess whether he or she is well-placed as a Christian.

THE PROVISION OF REMEMBRANCE

The prodigal son strayed from home but remembered the life of plenty with his father. Similarly, Naomi left Bethlehem with her husband in time of famine, but she remembered friends back home. Also, during the insurrection of Absalom, King David found refuge in a cave and uttered the words "Oh for a drink of water from Bethlehem's well." Remembrance is a powerful provision of God, if properly heeded. Remembrance has that great power to set you on God's pathway. Paul's admonition to young Timothy is a good example:

> When I call to remembrance the unfeigned faith
> that is in thee, which dwelt first in in thy grandmother
> Lois, and thy mother Eunice; and I am persuaded that
> is in thee also. Wherefore I put these in remembrance
> that thou stir up the gift of God, which is in the by
> the putting on of my hands (2 Timothy 1:5-6).

Jesus invoked the provision of remembrance of end times, recounting the experience of Lot's family in Sodom;

> Remember Lot's wife (Luke17:32).

The provision of remembrance takes on the form of punishment to those who spend eternity in hell in their unsaved condition. We recall the rich man's plea from hell to Father Abraham for mercy, whereupon the rich man was given this reply:

> But Abraham said, Son, remember that thou in thy life time receivedst thy good things, and likewise Lazarus evil things: but now he is comforted, and thou are tormented. (Luke 16:25)

THE PROVISION FOR RETURN AND REPENTANCE

Pride is an important obstacle to any prodigal returning to a healthy relationship with God and Christian friends. This can be a difficult hurdle. The prodigal son had to hear from his whining brother, and Naomi had to face the gossiping neighbors.

THE PROVISION FOR RECEPTION AND RECONCILATION

We are familiar with the return from the far county by both the prodigal son and Naomi. These welcoming graces highlight the words of Jesus:

> …I will in no wise cast out.

You may sometimes go into a far country in your thoughts, and possibly in your actions. You may be lured off course to become one of God's prodigals, i.e., out-of- place. Be open to introspection. The great old hymn of the Church, *Softly and Tenderly,* (Will Thompson, 1880) still speaks to wanderers.

> Oh, for the wonderful love he has promised,
> Promised for you and for me;

Though we have sinned, He has mercy and pardon,
Pardon for you and for me.

Refrain:
Come home, come home,
You who are weary, come home;
Earnestly, tenderly, Jesus is calling,
Calling, O sinner, come home!

The House Of Prisoners

… that opened not the house of his prisoners? (Isaiah 14:17).

Surely, such are the dwellings of the wicked, and this is the place of him that knoweth not God (Job 18:21).

I wish to bring these two Scriptures together, in a complementary manner, to learn more about the house of prisoners.

The house of prisoners of Isaiah 14:17 has an owner, who is identified in Isaiah 14:12. His name is Lucifer__ more commonly known as Satan.

How art thou fallen from heaven O Lucifer, son of the morning! how are thou cut down, which didst weaken the nations!

The house of prisoners is the biblical place of hell, and ultimately the Lake of Fire. I make these assertions from Job 18:21 about the house of prisoners:

- It depicts Satan's kingdom house
- It tells of the Satan's power over the unsaved

- It identifies one of Satan's house rules
- It recognizes Satan's nameless captives

Where is this house of prisoners? Jesus spoke of the "gates of hell" (Matthew 16:18). Is there a literal gated-kingdom, or is the language only figurative? Is it a place where the gates swing in only one direction?

In Job 18 the patriarch painted a foreboding word-picture of the house of prisoners. This Scripture is not uplifting, not pleasant, not an inspiration for songs. Perhaps, not to be read frequently. But it is part of the Bible record. The Christian recourse is to, all the more, appreciate Jesus and Heaven.

A literary obstacle must be overcome in understanding Job 18. The obstacle is the deferral of the subject of the discourse until the last verse of the chapter. Because the subject of the discourse____ "this is the place of him that knoweth not God" __is presented at the end of Chapter 18, we are intuitively prompted to begin earlier in those Scriptures to learn specifics about the house of prisoners.

WHERE THE SPIRIT IS DESTROYED

> Yea, the light of the wicked shall be put out, and the
> spark of his fire shall not shine. The light shall be dark
> in his tabernacle, and his candle shall be put out with
> him (Job 18:6,7).

God's supermax awaits the proud individual who rejects Jesus as Savior and Lord. That arrogant spirit, that I-can-make-it-on-my-own attitude will be snuffed out like a candle flame.

> The spirit of a man is the candle of the Lord (Proverbs
> 20:27).

We may recall the account of the rich man and Lazarus (Luke 16), that the rich man expressed no desire to be free of the house of prisoners. His spirit was subdued.

WHERE MOVEMENT IS RESTRICTED

The steps of his strength shall be straitened (Job 18:7).

The house of prisoners will be the stopping place for those who find petty excuses to run from the Lord and his Church. The Hebrew meanings for straitened are distressed and vexed.

WHERE CONFUSION ABOUNDS

His own counsel shall cast him down. For he is cast into a net by his own snare (Job 18:7-8).

Since God is not the author of confusion, little wonder that Satan's house of prisoners is filled with bewilderment (1 Corinthians 14:33).

WHERE STRENGTH IS GONE

The gin shall take him by the heel, and the robber shall prevail against him. The snare is laid for him in the ground, and a trap for him in the way (Job 18:9-10). His strength shallbe hungerbitten, and destruction shall be ready at his side (Job 18:12).

A "gin" was a horsehair, used to snare small birds. The metaphor accents the weakness of those in the house of prisoners.

WHERE CONFIDENCE IS ROOTED OUT

His confidence shall be rooted out of his tabernacle. (Job 18:14).

WHERE THE UNSAVED ULTIMATELY MEET SATAN

His confidence shall be rooted out of his tabernacle, and it shall bring him to the king of terrors (Job 18:14).

All they that know thee among the people shall be astonished at thee: thou shall be a terror, and never shalt thou be any more (Ezekiel 28:19).

WHEREIN IS FIRE AND BRIMSTONE

Brimstone shall be scattered upon his habitation (Job 18:15).

And the devil that deceived them was cast into the lake of fire and brimstone, where the beast and false prophet are, and shall be tormented day and night for ever and ever (Revelation 20:10).

And I saw the dead, small and great, stand before God; and the books were opened: and another book was opened, which is the book of life: and the dead were judged out of those things which were written in the books, according to their works. And the sea gave up the dead which were in it; and death and hell delivered up the dead which were in them; and they were judged every man according to their works. And death and hell were cast into the lake of fire. This is the second death (Revelation 20:12-14).

WHERE NAMES ARE FORGOTTON

His remembrance shall perish from the earth, and he shall have no name in the street (Job 18:17).

This is the answer to those who often wonder if, in Heaven, unsaved loved ones will be remembered.

WHERE KINSHIPS HAVE NO MEANING

He shall have neither son nor nephew among his people, nor any remaining in his dwellings (Job 18:19).

WHERE NEWCOMERS WILL BE SURPRISED

They that come after him shall be astonished at his day, as they that went before were affrighted (Job 18:20).

What a tragedy __ to pass this life and to be sadly surprised at the next!

The Lordship Of Christ

And as he journeyed, he came near Damascus: and suddenly there shined round about him a light from heaven: And he fell to the earth, and heard a voice saying, Saul, Saul, why persecutest thou me? And he said, Who art thou, Lord? And the Lord said, I am Jesus whom thou persecutest: it is hard for thee to kick against the pricks. And he trembling and astonished said, Lord, what wilt thou have me do ?(Acts 9:3-6).

THE NEW RELATIONSHIP

Saul's conversion experience on the Damascus Road is well recognized in Christendom. An immediate indication of the genuineness of his transformation may be gleaned from his question:

Lord, what will thou have me do?

The question was not the following:

What wilt thou have me do, Lord?

The latter question entails doing something, an activity, being busy____ in short, works. Is works the heart of Christianity?

Saul's question, **beginning** with "Lord", recognized a new relationship. This new relationship was not one of doing things. Indeed, he did not know what to do, until instructed by his new Lord.

WORKS, OR LORDSHIP?

Jesus set the correct priority of Lordship first, then works afterward in the following discourse.

> And why call ye me, Lord, Lord, and do not the things which I say? Whosoever cometh to me, and heareth my sayings, and doeth them, I will shew you to whom he is like: He is like a man which built an house, and digged deep, and laid the foundation on a rock: and when the flood arose, the stream beat vehemently upon that house, and could not shake it: for it was founded upon a rock. And he that heareth, and doeth not, is like a man that without a foundation built a house upon the earth; against which the stream eat vehemently, and immediately it fell; and the ruin of the house was great (Luke 6:46-49).

Do not the above verses teach that a relationship with Christ, which denies his Lordship, is like a house without a foundation?

JESUS IS BOTH SAVIOR AND LORD

Society may sometimes welcome Jesus as Savior, but slight him as Lord. For example, the familiar verse from Luke 2 may emphasize the role of Savior to some, while diminishing his role as Lord.

> For unto you is born this day in the city of David a savior, which is Christ the Lord.

The frequent usage of the two words, Savior and Lord, give weight to the Lordship of Christ.

	New Testament	**Book of Acts**
Savior	24	2
Lord	522	92

BELIEVING IN CHRIST, AND ACCEPTING HIS LORDSHIP

A shallow religious belief in Christ has been perpetuated throughout the church age. Only time in eternity will reveal meaningless confessions, empty emotional assents, and manipulations of popular verses_____ as opposed to a life-changing "born again" relationship.

The word, believe, used throughout most of the New Testament is translated from the Greek as **pisteuo.** It can serve as a powerful and wonderful word which leads to eternal life. But, without a life-changing transformation, it can also deceive the mind and spirit, deny the Lordship of Jesus Christ, and result in eternal damnation.

It will be recalled that demon spirits acknowledged Jesus as the Son of God.

> And when he was come to the other side of the country of the Gergesenes, there met him two possessed with devils, coming out of the tombs, exceeding fierce, so that no man might pass by that way. And, behold, they cried out, Saying, What have we to do with thee, Jesus, thou Son of God? Art thou come hither to torment us before the time (Matthew 8: 28,29)?

IS JESUS YOUR LORD?

The Prophet Isaiah provides the sharpest answer.

> O LORD our God, other lords have had dominion over us: but by thee only will we make mention of thy name (Isaiah 26:13).

There is one LORD, but many Lords.

The Unlived Life

And after these things I heard a great voice of much people, saying, Alleluia; Salvation, and glory, and honour, and power, unto the Lord our God (Revelation 19:1).

WE HAVE JUST BEGUN TO LIVE

So much lies ahead. Revelation 19:1 lists some waymarks of our future joys__ salvation, glory, honor and power of the unlived life.

MULTITUDES IN THE HEAVENLY LIFE

We can almost hear the united voice of the multitudes described in Revelation 19:1. The Heavenly throng is also described in Revelation 7:9.

> After this I beheld, and, lo, a great multitude, which no man could number, of all nations, and tongues, stood before the throne, clothed with white robes, and palms in their hands;

Our Lord spoke about the size of the throng in Luke 13:22-24.

> And he went through the cities and villages, teaching,
> and journeying toward Jerusalem. Then said one unto
> him, Lord, are there few that be saved? And he said
> unto them, Strive to enter in at the strait gate: for
> many, I say unto you, will seek to enter in, and shall
> not be able.

We should not be overly concerned about the population of
Heaven, as numbers might run counter to the biblical invitation
of "whosoever will." How inviting are the words of Jesus in Luke
14:22-23.

> And the servant said, Lord it is done as thou hast
> commanded, and yet there is room. And the Lord said
> unto his servant, Go out into the highways and hedges,
> and compel them to come in, that my house may be filled.

At this present time, there is, thankfully, room in Heaven. Yet,
in our future life, the Lord's house will be filled.

The Heavenly life will be one of righteousness, rather than of
numbers. This might be inferred from Abraham's challenging the
Lord, over the possibility of destroying Sodom Gomorrah (Genesis 18).

There is an implicit sadness about the message of Revelation 19:1.
If there is a voice of much people, then where are the other voices?

OUR UNLIVED SALVATION

We have only begun our salvation experience while here on
earth. Perhaps the disciple John's frequent address to us as "little
children" deserves more thought.

During our limited years here, we are privileged to experience
regeneration, whereby we are eternally saved and secure. And here

we also experience sanctification, whereby God's Spirit shapes us after his will; [(however, our sanctification does not leave us "without spot or wrinkle" (Ephesians 5:27) until we stand before the Judgement Seat of Christ (2 Corinthians 5:10)].

The greater part of our salvation is yet unlived. Glorification awaits. Only a few verses are necessary to excite us of the infancy of our salvation

> But as it is written, Eye hath not seen, nor ear heard, neither have entered into the heart of man, the things which God hath prepared for them that love him (1 Corinthians 2:9).

> But God, who is rich in mercy, for his great love wherewith he loved us, Even when we were dead in sins, hath quickened us together with Christ, (by grace ye are saved) And hath raised us up together, and made us to sit together in heavenly places in Christ Jesus: That in the ages to come he might shew the exceeding riches of his grace in his kindness toward us through Christ Jesus Ephesians 2:4-7).

OUR UNLIVED GLORY

Here on earth, we know hardly anything about divine glory. It seems just a word__ occasionally misused for worldly accomplishments. However, our future unlived lives will be all glorious.

Our meditation looks in two directions to describe our unlived glory. First, there should be adequate Scriptures which support our future glorification. Secondly, we should discover hints from the Bible which provide, at least meager, discernment of our glorified body.

DO SCRIPTURES TEACH OF FUTURE GLORIFICATION?

> The Spirit itself beareth witness with our spirit, that
> we are the children of God: And if children, then
> heirs; heirs of God, and joint-heirs with Christ; if
> so be that we suffer with him, that we may also be
> glorified together.For I reckon that the sufferings of
> this present time are not worthy to be compared to
> the glory which shall be revealed in us (Romans
> 8:16-18).

The above verses inform us that children of God will be
glorified____ together. This sense of "togetherness" harmonizes with
the description of the Rapture, (1 Corinthians 15:51).

The above Scripture also instructs us that our future glorified
bodies will exceed any comparison with our mortal bodies. In the
following Scripture Paul elevated the grandeur of our glorified bodies
to that of the galaxies

> There are also celestial bodies, and bodies terrestrial:
> but the **glory** of the celestial is one, and the **glory** of
> the terrestrial is another. There is one **glory** of the
> sun, and another **glory** of the moon, and another
> **glory** of the stars: for one star differeth from another
> star in **glory**. So is the resurrection of the dead. It is
> sown in corruption; it is raised in incorruption. It is
> sown in dishonour; it is raised in **glory**:_it is sown
> in weakness; it is raised in power (1 Corinthians 15:
> 40-43).

Three key words emerge from an examination of the above
underlined words: CREATED, UNIQUE AND BEAUTIFUL.

The cited objects were each created, inferring that God, who created us in his own image, will act in our glorification.

Additionally, the cited objects are unique, both in individual characteristics and in their distinctiveness from each other. We thrill at the words of Paul in 1 Corinthians 13:12, which informs that we will uniquely know others from this life.

> For now, we see through a glass darkly; but then face
> to face: now I know in part; but then shall I know
> even as also I am known.

Furthermore, we must readily admit that each of the created galactic bodies has a majestic beauty, as part of their uniqueness. We should anticipate that all glorified saints will possess a special beauty, provided by Christ.

> For our conversation (citizenship) is in heaven; from
> whence also we look for the Saviour, the Lord Jesus
> Christ: who shall change our vile body, that it may
> be fashioned like unto his glorious body, according
> to the working whereby he is able even to subdue all
> things unto himself (Philippians 3:20-21).

The above verses provide information, from which we glean the following: (1) that our earthly bodies are vile, the Greek interpretation meaning hollow or vain, (2) that our glorified bodies will be fashioned like the glorious body of Christ, (3) that Christ will be the one who changes our vile bodies, and (4) that our glorious transformation will be performed by Christ, simply because he is able to subdue all things to himself, i.e., all things obedient to Christ's will (Psalms 8:6).

Behold, what manner of love the Father hath bestowed upon us, that we should become the sons of God:therefore the world knoweth us not, because it knew him not. Beloved, now are we the sons of God, and it doeth not yet appear what we shall be: but we know that, when he shall appear, we shall be like him; for we shall see him as he is (1 John 3:1-2).

From John's Epistle we note: (1) that our sonship is bestowed on us by the love of God (2) that, at this present time, we are unsure of the details of our glorified bodies (3) that our change will occur at the appearance of Christ (4) that we will, in some manner, be like Christ, and (5) that Christ will be recognizable.

INSIGHTS TO OUR GLORIFICATION FROM CHRIST'S POST-RESURRECTION BODY

Thoughts of our future glorification leave us with much curiosity about the nature of our new body. Glorification will be the final divine act of our redemptive salvation.

We may gain some understanding about our glorified body by making observations about the body of Christ, following his resurrection.

However, we emphasize that the resurrection body will be different from that of the glorified body__ if in no other respect, but that the latter radiates brightness. The brightness of glorification will be discussed later.

First, Christ's post- resurrection body was a physical, touchable, body, with visible features that enabled him (1) to be recognizable (2) to be receptive to eating (see John 21) __ perhaps as fellowship (3) to have memory of events and people before his crucifixion.

Secondly, the post-resurrection body of Christ was unique in that he retained the open wounds of his crucifixion, and that he entered a room without opening the door.

> But Thomas, one of the twelve, called Didymus, was not with them when Jesus came. The other disciples therefore said unto him, We have seen the Lord. But he said unto them, Except I shall see in his hands the print of the nails, and put my finger into the print of the nails, and thrust my hand into his side, I will not believe. And after eight days again his disciples were within, and Thomas with them: then came Jesus, the doors being shut, and stood in the midst, and said, Peace be unto you. Then said he to Thomas, Reach hither thy finger, and behold my hands; and reach hither thy hand, and thrust it into my side: and be not faithless, but believing (John 20: 24-27).

Thirdly, Christ had the ability to appear, and to reappear elsewhere, at his will (Mark 16:14). This suggests that he was not limited by time or distance in traversing different locations. Additionally, Christ's ascension, recorded in Acts 1:9, suggests that he had power over earth's gravitational force. Each Christian will likewise experience this power over time, distance and gravity during the Rapture, i.e., reflect on the meaning of "twinkling of an eye" in 1 Corinthians 15:52.

Fourthly, the post- resurrection body of Jesus was without blood. His open wounds revealed that he obviously did not possess a functioning circulation system. That he was without blood might be inferred from his remarks in Luke 24:39.

> Behold my hands and my feet, that it is I myself: handle me, and see; for a spirit hath not flesh and bones, as ye see me have.

Instead of saying flesh and blood, he characterized his body as flesh and bone. That glorified bodies will be without blood, might also be inferred from 1 Corinthians 15:50.

> Now this I say, brethren, that flesh and blood cannot inherit the kingdom of God: neither doth corruption inherit incorruption.

In our earthly life, the following is true;

> For the life of the flesh is in the blood (Leviticus 17:11).

However, in the Heavenly sphere, life will be manifested by light. Light will replace blood.

> In him was life; and the life was the light of men (John 1:4).

> And there shall be no night there; and they need no candle, neither light of the sun; for the Lord God giveth them light (Revelation 22:5).

God's people will be "children of light" (Luke 16:8), not blood.

THE RESURRECTION BODY AND THE GLORIFIED BODY

Unlike the resurrection body, the glorified body emanates physical brightness. That the resurrection body was without unusual brightness is evident from the following incidents.

- When our resurrected Savior stood on the shores by the Sea of Tiberias and asked the distant disciples if they had any fish

(John 21), there was no evident brightness mentioned in that Scripture.

- Likewise, when the resurrected Christ made appearances to his disciples there was no evident brightness.
- Also, the two men on the Emmaus Road unknowingly entertained our resurrected Lord, but there is no record of any unusual brightness (Luke 24).
- While the resurrected Savior was taken up in the clouds (Acts 1), there was no mention of any special brightness.

THE LITERAL BRIGHTNESS OF CHRIST, GLORIFIED

The literal brightness of Jesus was observed by Peter, James and John, when led by Jesus to a meeting with Moses and Elijah on Mt. Hermon, recorded in Luke 9. Although Jesus was yet in his earthly body__ and obviously neither resurrected nor glorified___ his **temporal** glorification (verse 32) was a visual message to Moses and Elijah of good things to come.

> And it came to pass about an eight days after these sayings, he took Peter and John and James, and went up into a mountain to pray. And as he prayed, the fashion of his countenance was altered, and his raiment was white and glistening (Luke 9:28,29). But Peter and they that were with him were heavy with sleep: and when they were awake, they saw his glory, and the two men that stood by him (Luke 9:32).

Both Moses and Elijah had previously experienced a revelation from God (see Exodus 33 and 1 Kings 19) on this mountain, from which Moses had made the following request:

> And he said, I beseech thee, shew me thy glory
> (Exodus 33:18).

To this request the Lord replied,

> Thou canst not see my face: for there shall no man see
> me, and live (Exodus 33:20).

Following this request, Moses was called to Mount Sinai, where he received the Ten Commandments. Moses descended the mountain with a visible brightness from his encounter with the Lord (Exodus 34:29-30, 2 Corinthians 3:7).

> And it came to pass, when Moses came down from
> mount Sinai with the two tablets of testimony in
> Moses' hand, when he came down from the mount,
> that Moses wist not that the skin of his face shone
> while he talked with him. And when Aaron and all
> the children of Israel saw Moses, behold, the skin of
> his face shone; and they were afraid to come nigh him.

Was there something mesmerizing to the human eye about the **glorified** brightness of Christ? Yes. Vivid, physical instances are described from the following Scriptural accounts.

The salvation of Saul on the Damascus Road was attended by a literal blinding light____ "above the brightness of the sun" (Acts 26:13) __ which emanated from the glorified Christ (Acts 9). Saul was blind for three days.

In another instance of Christ's brightness, John, on the Isle of Patmos, declared these words:

And his countenance was as the sun shineth in his strength. And when I saw him, I fell at his feet as dead (Revelation 1:16-17).

This same physical light from Jesus, blinding to Saul, is prophesized to be a catastrophic power to the Antichrist at the last war (Armageddon).

For the mystery of iniquity doth already work: only he who now letteth will let, until he be taken out of the way. And then shall that Wicked be revealed, whom the Lord shall consume with the spirit of his mouth, and shall destroy with the brightness of his coming (2 Thessalonians 2:7-8).

The gruesome effects of this destructive light from our glorified Christ are described in Zechariah 14:12.

And this shall be the plague wherewith the LORD will smite all the people that have fought against Jerusalem; Their flesh shall consume away as they stand upon their feet, and their eyes shall consume away in their holes, and their tongue shall consume away in their mouth.

The Zechariah 14:12 Scripture leaves little doubt that the destructive effect of Christ's brightness will be instantaneous, i.e., the enemies will be yet standing.

The word "consume" is used in the Zechariah 14:12 Scripture. The Hebrew transliteration is *maqaq*, meaning, to melt.

The word "consume" is also used in the 2 Thessalonians 2 description of Christ's brightness. In this instance, the Greek transliteration is the word *analisko*.

Most revealing is the fact that, in the New Testament Scriptures, this word, **analisko,** for consume was used in only one other instance, Luke 9:54.

> And when his disciples James and John saw this, they said,
> Lord wilt thou that we command fire to come down from
> heaven, and consume *(analisko)*them, even as Elias did?

The reference to Elijah is the familiar account of the destruction of the altars of Baal, on which fire from the Lord fell and utterly consumed that site (1 Kings 18:38).

The brightness of Jesus is two-fold in nature. First, the spiritual light of Christ manifests itself as spiritual conviction, whereby sinners are drawn to the saving knowledge of Christ. Secondly, the light of the glorified Christ is a physical light.

Revelation 21:23 states that the new Jerusalem city of God will be powered by the light of Jesus.

> And the city had no need of the sun, neither of the
> moon, to shine in it: for the glory of God did lighten
> it, and the Lamb is the light thereof.

God's special light was created three days before the establishment of sunlight (Genesis 1:3).

The literal brightness of our glorified Christ may have been foreseen by Old Testament prophets, although the distinction between spiritual and physical brightness may not clear from every Scripture.

The prophet Habakkuk foresaw the coming "Holy One", and declared

> His glory covered the heavens, and the earth was
> full of his praise. And his brightness was as the light
> (Habakkuk 3:3-4).

Isaiah's prophecy is cited in Matthew 4:16, concerning Jesus.

> The people which sat in darkness saw great light; and to
> them which sat in the region of shadow of death light is
> sprung up.

THE LITERAL BRIGHTNESS OF ANGELS

Various Scriptures describe angels of God in bright or shining
appearances (Daniel 10:6, Matthew 28:2-5, Luke 24:4 and Acts
10:30).

Revelation 18:1 is especially interesting in describing the angelic
brightness.

> And after these things I saw another angel come down
> from heaven, having great power; and the earth was
> lightened with his glory.

The context is clearly a physical brightness. Is it safe to assume
that the brightness will not be over all of the earth, but rather local???

The appearance of the fallen angel Lucifer (Satan) is of special
interest. If Satan could be visibly seen, for example like the angels at
Christ's tomb, then this created angel would also emanate physical
brightness, like other angels. This light of Satan is noted in 2
Corinthians 10:14.

> And no marvel; for Satan himself is transformed into an
> angel of light.

> Therefore, it is no great thing if his ministers also be
> transformed as the ministers of righteousness; whose
> end shall be according to their works (2 Corinthians
> 11:15).

The deceptiveness of Satan is that his earthly ministers may outwardly appear to be light-bearers, or righteous.

THE ORIGIN AND POWER OF GLORIFIED BRIGHTNESS

The origin of Christ's glorified brightness is God, the Father, as underlined in the following Scripture from Hebrews 1.

> God, who at sundry times and in divers manners spake in times past unto the fathers by the prophets, hath in these last days spoken unto us by his Son, whom he hath appointed heir of all things, by whom also he made the worlds; **who being the brightness of his glory**, and the express image of his person.

A natural question is how will God "regulate" this brightness in the unlived life_____ recalling the biblical incidences of (1) a glow on Moses' face (2) temporary blindness of Saul (3) death symptoms of John (4) destruction of an invading army, and (5) future replacement of the sun?

The degree of brightness may have much to do with conditions of righteousness versus condemnation. This is only a partial explanation, deduced from Moses' receiving the Ten Commandments__ which brought condemnation under the Law.

> But if the ministration of death, written and engraven in stones, was glorious, so that the children of Israel could not steadfastly behold the face of Moses for the glory of his countenance; which glory was to be done away: How shall not the ministration of the spirit be rather glorious? (Hebrews 3:7-8)

Those who influence others to a saving knowledge of Christ will be imbued with distinct brightness (Daniel 12:3).

They that be wise (teachers) shall shine as the
brightness of the firmament; and they that turn many
to righteousness as the stars for ever and ever.

OUR UNLIVED HONOR

The children of God, in glorified bodies, will be honored with
rewards in Heaven. In giving his beatitudes (Matthew 5) Christ
concluded:

Rejoice, and be exceeding glad: for great is your
reward in heaven.

Christ conditioned his rewards on deeds performed.

And, behold, I come quickly; and my reward is with
me, to give every man according as his work shall be
(Revelation 22:12).

The language seems clear, that Christ will give rewards in the
unlived life, and that the nature of those rewards (beyond the scope
our meditation) will be based on each saint's labors.

Look to yourselves, that we lose not those things
which we have wrought, but that we receive a full
reward (2 John 8).

The above Scripture suggests that some saints may come short of
a full reward. The following may be a factual example

Alexander the coppersmith did me much evil: the
Lord reward him according to his works (2 Timothy
4:14).

Paul enlarged on the restrictions of future rewards in 1 Corinthians 3:13–15.

> Every man's work shall be made manifest: for the day shall declare it, because it shall be revealed by fire; and the fire shall try every man's work of what sort it is. If any man's work abide which he hath built thereupon, he shall receive a reward. If any man's work shall be burned, he shall suffer loss: but he himself shall be saved; yet so as by fire.

The above verses instruct that a saint may lose rewards, likely to be given at the time of the Judgement Seat of Christ (2 Corinthians 5:10). The references to fire in the above verses speak of judgement, as suggested in the following Scripture.

> Wherefore we receiving a kingdom which cannot be moved, let us have grace, whereby we may serve God acceptably with reverence and godly fear: For our God is a consuming fire (Hebrew 12:28,29).

OUR UNLIVED POWER

Glorification will transform our body into one like that of Christ. Our new body will be one of power.

> For our conversation(citizenship) is in heaven; from whence we look for the Saviour, the Lord Jesus Christ: Who shall change our vile body, that it may be fashioned like unto his glorious body, according to the working whereby he is able even to subdue all things unto himself (Philippians 3:20-21).

It is sown in dishonour; it is raised in glory:_it is
sown in weakness; it is raised in power (1 Corinthians
15: 43).

The raising and glorifying of Christian bodies will first include
those who have died in Christ since the beginning of the Church
Age, followed by the glorifying of Christians who are alive at his
coming.

For this we say unto you by the word of the Lord,
that we which are alive and remain unto the coming
of the Lord shall not prevent them which are asleep.
For the lord himself shall descend from heaven with
a shout, with the voice of the archangel, and with the
trump of God: and the dead in Christ shall rise first:
Then we which are alive and remain shall be caught
up together with them in the clouds, to meet the
Lord in the air: and so shall we ever be with the Lord.
Wherefore comfort one another with these words (1
Thessalonians 4:15-18).

The two words "caught up" describe our rapturous ascension. In
1 Corinthians 15:51 we are informed that Christians will be changed
during the Rapture. They will be both resurrected and glorified
simultaneously, to ever be with the Lord.

The power of our glorified body will be manifest in at least
two ways (1) in performing bodily activities like those of our post-
resurrected Lord (1 John 3:2), and (2) in having special leadership
roles over the surviving nations of people (and their posterity),
following the Tribulation.

THE TRIBULATION

The Rapture of the Church will be followed by deception and turmoil on earth, over a seven-year period, called the Tribulation. The prophet Jeremiah called it "the time of Jacob's trouble" (Jeremiah 30:7). Jesus called it "the beginning of sorrows." (Matthew 24:8) and referred to the last half as one of great tribulation.

> For then shall be great tribulation, such as was not since the beginning of the world to this time, no, nor ever shall be (Matthew 24:21).

Isaiah urged the saints to go into hiding, and Zechariah (14:5) mentioned a specific hiding place.

> Come, my people, enter thou into thy chambers, and shut thy doors about thee: hide thyself as it were for a little moment, until the indignation be overpast (Isaiah 26:20).

The Tribulation will end with the Armageddon War, where 83.4 percent of the invading enemies of Israel will be destroyed (Ezekiel 39:1-2).

> Therefore, thou son of man, prophesy against Gog, and say, Thus saith the Lord God; Behold, I am against thee, O Gog, the chief prince of Meshech and Tubal: And I will turn thee back, and leave but the sixth part of thee, and will cause thee to come from the north parts, and will bring thee upon the mountains of Israel:

The context of the statistic of one-sixth survivors should be logically analyzed. In terms of mathematical percentages, one-sixth is equivalent to 16.6 percent. It seems illogical that this implies that 83.4 percent of the world's population will be destroyed, since that population would include infants, children, women and older people. Rather, the 16.6 percent who survive should, quite logically, apply to the number of the invading army__ not the population of the world at the time. Therefore, if the invading army should number, for example one million, then 166,000 would survive, while 834,000 would perish. Whatever the size of the invading army, the population of the world would still be large, perhaps in the billions.

The above exercise with the 16.6 percent survival is presented to counteract the opinions of some, that all sinners would perish by the end of the Tribulation, and that only saints would live during the Millennium. On the contrary, large numbers of infants, children, women, older people, handicapped, along with the 16.6 percent survivors of the invading army, will enter the Millennium. These are the unbelieving mortals of the Millennium, along with their posterity. Their mortal presence will give rise to such phrases as "judgement of the nations", and Christ "ruling with a "rod of iron." To over-emphasize the point, if only believers lived during the Millennium, then what would be the explanation for Christ ruling believers with a rod of iron?

Whatever the numerical size of the invading army, approximately 85-percent of that number will be destroyed, by the "brightness" of Christ's coming (2 Thessalonians 2:7-8) ____ leaving the following gruesome sight for seven years of burial details (Ezekiel 39), and supper for the fowls of the air (Revelation 19:8).

> And this shall be the plague wherewith the LORD
> will smite all the people that have fought against
> Jerusalem; Their flesh shall consume away as they
> stand upon their feet, and their eyes shall consume

away in their holes, and their tongue shall consume
away in their mouth (Zechariah 12:12).

Death will be horrific for many unbelievers when Christ returns
near the end of the Tribulation.

However, Revelation 6:9-11 teaches that all who become
believers in Christ during that seven- year period(Tribulation) will
be martyred, many by beheading (Revelation 20:4-6). These are
described as overcomers in Revelation Scriptures, i.e. "that should
be killed as they were." (in the following Scripture).

> And when he had opened the fifth seal, I saw under
> the altar the souls of them that were slain for the word
> of God, and for the testimony which they held: And
> they cried with a loud voice saying, How long, O
> Lord, holy and true, dost thou not judge and avenge
> our blood on them that dwell on the earth? And
> white robes were given unto every one of them; and
> it was said unto them that they should rest yet for a
> little season, until their fellow servants also and their
> brethren, that should be killed as they were, should
> be fulfilled (Revelation 6:9-11).

Christ spoke of these martyred overcomers in eight Revelation
Scriptures, and cited future blessings awaiting them. Two of the eight
Scriptures follow.

> And he that overcomes, and keepeth my works unto
> the end, to him will I give power over the nations
> (Revelation 2:26).

> He that overcometh shall not be hurt of the second
> death (Revelation 2:11).

THE FUTURE RESURRECTION OF OLD TESTAMENT SAINTS AND MARTYRS OF THE TRIBULATION

It is suggested that both the Old Testament saints and the martyrs of the Tribulation will both be resurrected and glorified at the same time, most likely following the martyrdom of Tribulation witnesses, i.e., after the "little season" cited in Revelation 6:9-11. The exact date for the resurrection of the Tribulation martyrs will likely be determined by the completion of all executions. Beheading will apparently be the manner of executions (Revelation 20:4-6), and this atrocity could be on a massive scale, as conditions become ominous for those who war against God. The barbaric nature of such executions should raise thoughts about those religions presently given to this practice.

The resurrection and glorification of the Old Testament saints will include those in Abraham's company (Luke 16), including John Baptist. A teaching of 1 Peter 3:18,19 has Christ journeying from his grave, by the power of the Holy Spirit, to Abraham and company, and preaching to those saints.

> For Christ also hath once suffered for sins, the just for the unjust, that he might bring us to God, being put to death in the flesh, but quickened by the Spirit. By which also, he went and preached to the spirits in prison.

The visit to Abraham and company harmonizes with the words of Jesus in John 8:56.

> Your father Abraham rejoiced to see my day: and saw it, and was glad.

Abraham made several prophetic statements during his day, which suggest a theophany. Some of his statements were:

51

- Shall not the Judge of all the earth do right (Genesis 18:25)
- God will provide a lamb (substitute for Isaac-Genesis 22:8)
- His discourse in Luke 16

The reference to "prison" in Peter's account harmonizes with the words of Paul in Ephesians 4:8.

> Wherefore he saith, When he ascended up on high,
> he led captivity captive, and gave gifts unto men.

On the day of his crucifixion, Christ's "prison preaching" (1 Peter 3:18,19) enabled believers to ascend from their Abrahamic abode into Paradise (12 Corinthians 12:4), into the presence of God.

Christ's ascension included that of the repentant thief on the cross.

> This day thou shalt be with me in paradise.

Needless to say, it was a busy time when Christ was laid in the tomb.

APPEARANCES FROM THE GRAVE

Special attention is warranted to consider several individuals who might appear to have been resurrected from the dead **before** Christ.

However, at the onset we insist that Christ was the first to be gloriously raised from the dead, according to 1 Corinthians 15:20

> But now is Christ risen from the dead, and become
> the firstfruits of them that slept.

Lazarus of Bethany and Jairus' daughter

These were miraculously raised from their dead state. However, each eventually died again.

Moses and Elijah on the Mount of Transfiguration, and saints rising from the grave (Matthew 27:42)

The meeting with Moses and Elijah has been generally well received by fundamental believers, especially since it was witnessed by three disciples, and included particulars of the approaching crucifixion.

However, Matthew's eye-catching statement, in two verses, of saints rising from their graves after Christ's death has raised a myriad of concerns, with "hand waving" explanations.

Some literary explanations might appear to be dismissive of Matthew's observation, since the Matthew 27 Scripture is not cited elsewhere in the Bible. But then, other gospel writers may not have wished to challenge the observation of the revered Matthew. Some weak attempts to support Matthew's observation make mention that the attending earthquake may have shattered some tombs. However, this view hardly explains how the tomb-dwellers went into town, or their eventual whereabouts.

I propose the following explanation for Matthew's observation, in combination with the appearance of Moses and Elijah on the Mount of Transfiguration.

1. That the Old Testament appearance of Moses and Elijah on the Mount of Transfiguration constituted an **appearance** from Abraham's world. Such appearances would be no more difficult for God than the appearance of the fourth man in the fire of Daniel 3:25, or the reappearance of dead Samuel to King Saul (1 Samuel 28:15). The latter appearance was not a resurrection.

2. That the Old Testament saints of Abraham's world were anxious for redemption from their estate, with a concern similar to that of the tribulation martyr's, i.e., "how long, O Lord, holy and true…?" (Revelation 6:10).

3. That Christ met with Moses and Elijah on the Mount of Transfiguration, with the encouragement that his approaching death on the cross, and resurrection, would signal the imminent resurrection of the saints.

4. That Christ's meeting with Moses and Elijah foreshadowed his approaching "preaching to the saints in prison" (1 Peter 3:18-19)

5. That the opening of graves and downtown parade of some Old Testament saints (Matthew 27:52-53) was a divinely approved **celebration**, of the complete resurrection from Abraham's world____ **subsequent** to Christ's resurrection. There was no recorded brightness of their persons, indicative of glorification. The brevity of their visit preceded their ascension and glorification.

6. That the meeting of Moses and Elijah with Christ on the Mount of Transfiguration may have included plans for later appearances to preach during the Tribulation (Revelation 11).

OUR POWER DURING THE MILLENNIUM

The climax of the Tribulation will coincide with major changes on the earth, along with the incarceration of Satan for 1000 years. During this time the earth will become the Kingdom of Christ, widely recognized in Christendom as the Millennium. Some of the dramatic changes will include:

- The removal of the seas (Revelation 21:1), which God had originally established (Genesis 1).
- The cleansing of the earth by fire (2 Peter 3:7-13; Luke 17:28-29; Luke 12:49; Malachi 4:1).
- The emergence of a new heaven, from its present location (wherever), said to be coming down to earth (Revelation

21:2-3). It is called new Jerusalem, stated to be holy. Is this a divine satellite?

- The replacement of the sun as a source of light for the Holy City (Revelation 21:23,25), wherein is no darkness.
- The cessation of light and darkness cycles on the earth, established by God (Genesis 1:14) __ perhaps removed because heavenly bodies have long been objects of worship (for example Ezekiel 8:16). The cessation of roles of these heavenly bodies is noted in many Scriptures, including Isaiah 60:19; Joel 3:15, Revelation 8; Matthew 24:29.

> The sun shall be no more thy light by day; neither for
> brightness shall the moon give light unto thee: but the
> LORD shall be unto thee an everlasting light, and thy
> God thy glory (Isaiah 60:19).

The emergence of a new source of light, described in Zechariah 14:6,7.

> And it shall come to pass in that day, that the light
> shall not be clear, nor dark: But it shall be one day
> which shall be known to the Lord, not day, nor night:
> but it shall come to pass, that at evening time it shall
> be light (Zechariah 14:6,7).

- The beginning of a different perspective of time. The present awe of extended years will fade, as earth's inhabitants adjust to God's view of time, cited metaphorically in the following:

> For a thousand years in thy sight are but as yesterday
> when it is past, and as a watch in the night (Psalms
> 90:4)

Peter chided personal ignorance of God's perspective of time (2 Peter 2:8):

> But, beloved, be not ignorant of this one thing, that one day is with the Lord as a thousand years, and a thousand years as a day (2 Peter 2:8).

The 1000 years of the Millennium are understood to be real earth- years. However, in a metaphorical sense, they would be nothing more than one of our earth days, by God's reckoning.

OUR POWER OVER DEATH

The experience of death during the 1000 years will continue on nations of unbelievers (and their posterity) who survive the Tribulation.

However, those who will not experience death will include (1) the raptured saints of the Church in their glorified bodies (2) the glorified Old Testament saints, and (3) the glorified martyrs of the Tribulation.

> And I saw thrones, and they that sat upon them, and judgement was given unto them: and I saw the souls of them that were beheaded for the witness of Jesus, and for the word of God, and which had not worshipped the beast, neither his image, neither had received his mark upon their foreheads, or in their hands; and they lived and reigned with Christ a thousand years. But the rest of the dead lived not again until the thousand years were finished. This is the first resurrection. Blessed and holy is he that hath part in the first resurrection: on such the second death hath no power, but they shall be priests of God and

of Christ, and shall reign with him a thousand years
(Revelation 20:4-6).

It may be well to emphasize some of the main points of the above
Scripture.

- Tribulation martyrs (believers in Christ) will be slain during
  the Tribulation, but afterwards will be resurrected, and will
  have priestly power during the Millennium of Christ's reign
  on earth. These are blessed and holy ones__ overcomers, by
  virtue of martyrdom. They will die no more. They are part
  of the first resurrection.
- Contrary to the Tribulation martyrs, there will be large
  numbers of the Tribulation who will not receive Christ, i.e.,
  "the number of whom is as the sand of the sea" (Revelation
  20:8). Their physical deaths as mortals will transpire during
  the Millennium years; and the continuance of their death
  will remain until the end of the 1000 years. This means that
  anyone failing to trust Christ during the Millennium will die
  twice, in the following respects. The first death will occur
  naturally as a mortal, during the 1000 years. The second
  death will be eternal separation from God, described in the
  following verses.

And the sea gave up the dead which were in it; and
death and hell delivered up the dead which were in
them: and they were judged every man according to
his works. And death and hell were cast into the lake
of fire. This is the second death (Revelation 20:13-14).

He that overcometh shall inherit all things; and I
will be his God, and he shall be my son. But the

fearful, and unbelieving, and the abominable, and murderers, and whoremongers, and sorcerers, and idolaters, and all liars, shall have their part in the lake which burneth with fire and brimstone: which is the second death (Revelation 21:7-8).

- Later in this meditation we shall see that an age limit for salvation will be imposed on mortals who refuse to trust Christ, after living beyond 100 years during the Millennium (Isaiah 65:17-21).
- We should not read into Revelation 20:4-6 that Israel alone will rule and reign with Christ during the Millennium, because Revelation 5:7-10 states that all the redeemed will reign during Christ's kingdom.

And he came and took the book out of the right hand of him that sat upon the throne. And when he had taken the book, the four beasts and four and twenty elders fell down before the Lamb, having every one of them harps, and golden vials full of odours, which are the prayers of the saints. And they sung a new song, saying, Thou art worthy to take the book, and to open the seals thereof: fort thou wast slain, and hast redeemed us to God by thy blood out of every kindred, and tongue, and people, and nation; and hast made us unto our God kings and priests: and we shall reign on the earth.

Jesus spoke on several occasions of future positions of power, to be filled by select persons in his kingdom.

And Jesus said unto them, Verily I say unto you, that ye which have followed me, in the regeneration when the Son of man shall sit in the throne of his glory, ye shall also sit upon twelve thrones, judging the twelve tribes of Israel (Matthew 19:28).

QUESTIONS FOR 1000 YEARS OF UNLIVED LIFE

QUESTION #1

During the 1000 years on earth will there be a mixed multitude" (Exodus 12:38) of both glorified and mortal individuals?

ANSWER

Yes. There will be the raptured and glorified saints of the Church, which will include all who have trusted in Jesus, i.e., those from the beginning of Christ's Church to those alive at the time of the Rapture.

> For this I say unto you by the word of the Lord, that we which are alive and remain unto the coming of the Lord shall not prevent them which are asleep. For the Lord himself shall descend from heaven with a shout, with the voice of the archangel, and with the trump of God: and the dead in Christ shall rise first (1 Thessalonians 4:15-16).

Secondly, there will be the martyred believers of the Tribulation (Revelation 20:4,6), who will have glorified bodies.

Thirdly, the glorified saints of the Old Testament period, through the thief on the cross (Daniel 12:1-3,) will be present in glorified bodies.

Coexisting with these glorified saints will be hordes of unbelievers of all nations. These are the 16.6 percent survivors (one sixth) of the invading army against Israel (Ezekiel 39:2), in addition to the surviving at-large population of infants, children, women, etc. of that time.

> And it shall come to pass, that every one that is left of all the nations which came against Jerusalem shall even go up from year to year to worship the King, the Lord of hosts, and to keep the feast of tabernacles. And it shall be, that whoso will not come up of all the families of the earth unto Jerusalem to worship the King, the Lord of hosts, even upon them shall be no rain (Zechariah 14:16-17).

> Therefore, thou son of man, prophesy against Gog, and say, Thus saith the Lord God; Behold, I am against thee, O Gog, the chief prince of Meshech and Tubal: And I will turn thee back, and leave but the sixth part of thee, and will cause thee to come from the north parts, and will bring thee upon the mountains of Israel (Ezekiel 39:1-2).

QUESTION #2

Will the 1000- year period be "heaven on earth"?

ANSWER

No. The multitude of surviving mortals will have sinful hearts. Those who do not trust in Christ will experience everlasting second death (Revelation 20:13-14).

QUESTION #3

What is the purpose of the rule and reign of Christ for 1000 years?

ANSWER

The shortest answer lies in the statement of Abraham, from Genesis 18:25.

Shall not the Judge of all the earth do right?

During the period of 1000 years, Christ will rule with a "rod of iron" (Revelation 2:27), but Revelation 20 informs that Satan will be temporarily loosed at the end of the 1000 years, and that he will deceive many__ "of whom is the sand of the sea" (Revelation 20:4). The time of the 1000- year reign of Christ might aptly be called the Judgement of the Nations.

From another viewpoint, the 1000-year period will present an opportunity of grace for children, innocently born during the Tribulation and the Millennium. During the Millennium such children will have opportunity to trust in the atoning blood of Christ. Otherwise, the following statement from Paul could not be true:

> For the grace of God that bringeth salvation hath appeared to all men (Titus2:11).

Without the 1000-year period, those children, born in innocence from the posterity of Tribulation survivors, would be deprived of grace, i.e., affirmed in Titus 2.

QUESTION #4

Will Christ's throne be located in Israel during the 1000-year reign?

ANSWER

Revelation 21:2-3 states that there will be a "new Jerusalem coming down". The present earth will be purified by fire (2 Peter 3:7-13; Luke 17:28-29). Some references as to "going up to Jerusalem" (Zechariah 14:16-17) might suggest that the new Heaven will be near, but not necessarily connected, to the earth.

QUESTION #5

Will Christ be seen throughout the earth during the 1000 years?

ANSWER

Christ will see, and he will also be visited. Firstly, he will see others because his glorified body has power over time and distance. As was true in his post-resurrection body, Christ may make appearances at will. Equally important, Christ will be both visited and worshiped by the surviving nations (Zechariah 14:16-17).

> It shall come to pass, that every one that is left of all nations which came against Jerusalem shall even go up from year to year to worship the King, the Lord of hosts, and to keep the feast of tabernacles. And it shall be, that whoso will not come up of all the families of the earth unto Jerusalem to worship the King, the Lord of hosts, even upon them shall be no rain (Zechariah 14:16-17.

QUESTION #6

What will inhabitants of the earth do during the 1000 years___ play harps and sing songs? Will they grow old?

ANSWER

Read LIFE DURING THE MILLENNIUM

QUESTION #7

Will Kingdom inhabitants have memories of the past?

ANSWER

There appears to be no reasons for memory lapse of those mortals surviving the Tribulation. These are survivors, but they will retain memory of their earthly rejection of Christ. A Kingdom requirement will be imposed on nations to regularly visit and worship Christ.

> And it shall come to pass, that every one that is left of all the nations which came against Jerusalem shall even go up from year to year to worship the King, the Lord of hosts, and to keep the feast of tabernacles (Zachariah 14:16).

The capacity of remembrance will be an eternal punishment to those who reject Jesus as Savior. Recall the response of Abraham to the rich man in hell.

> But Abraham said, Son, remember that thou in thy lifetime receivedst thy good things, and likewise Lazarus evil things: but now he is comforted, and thou are tormented (Luke 16:25).

The recall of past events may be a different matter for the glorified saints.

> For, behold, I create new heavens and a new earth: and the former shall not be remembered, nor come to mind (Isaiah 65:17).

There are those who assert that we will know more in the future than now, glorying in the old hymn "We'll understand it better by and by". Conversely, the bliss of the unlived life may completely overshadow this life's turmoil. It seems inconceivable that saints will be with the Lord, and not have awareness of the beginnings of their salvation. The following verse from Isaiah 11:9 seems conclusive:

> For the earth shall be full of the knowledge of the Lord, as the waters cover the sea.

We thrill at the words of Paul in 1 Corinthians 13:12:

> For now, we see through a glass darkly; but then face to
> face: now I know in part; but then shall I know even as
> also I am known.

QUESTION #8

How will so many inhabitants crowd into a finite earth during
the 1000 years? The earth seems over- populated now.

ANSWER

They will live on this earth because the seas will be removed
(Revelation 21:1), which will be a reversal of God's activity described
in Genesis 1. The seas cover more than ninety percent of the earth's
land area. Also, who is to say that other planets will not be habitable?

QUESTION #9

Why should Satan be incarcerated for 1000 years, only to be
released? He will always be a deceiver. What's the point of locking
him up, only to release him later?

ANSWER

One answer is to physically expose the sinful nature of unredeemed
mortal inhabitants. Multitudes will rebel against God when Satan
returns from 1000 years of incarceration. The end- time rebellion
adds meaning to the words of Jeremiah:

> The heart is deceitful above all things, and desperately
> wicked: who can know it? I the Lord search the heart,
> I try the reins, even to give every man according to
> his ways, and according to the fruit of his doings
> (Jeremiah 17:9-10).

And the devil that deceived them was cast into the lake of fire and brimstone, where the beast and false prophet are, and shall be tormented day and night for ever and ever. And I saw a great white throne, and him that sat on it, from whose face the earth and the heaven fled away; and there was found no place for them. And I saw the dead, small and great stand before God; and the books were open: and another book was open, which is the book of life: and the dead were judged out of those things which were written in the books, according to their works. And the sea gave up the dead, which were in it; and death and hell delivered up the dead which were in them: and they were judged every man according to their works. And death and hell were cast into the lake of fire. This is the second death. And whosoever was not found written in the book of life was cast into the lake of fire (Revelation 20:10-15).

LIFE DURING THE MILLENNIUM

MILLENNIUM OF UNLIMITED KNOWLEDGE

The earth shall be full of the knowledge of the Lord, as waters cover the sea (Isaiah 11:9).

But grow in grace, and in the knowledge of our Lord and Saviour Jesus Christ. To him be glory both now and forever. Amen (2 Peter 3:18).

We will never approach the depths of God's knowledge. Yet, very importantly, God is knowable. Equally so, we will never exhaust the depths of knowledge which he is able to impart to us through his Son.

Paul called it the "excellency of knowledge of Christ Jesus", and sought to further know Christ.

> Yea doubtless, and I count all things but loss for the excellency of the knowledge of Christ Jesus my Lord: for whom I have suffered the loss of all things, and do count them but dung, that I may win Christ. And be found in him, not having mine own righteousness, which is of the law, but that which is through the faith of Christ, the righteousness which is of God by faith: That I may know him, and the power of his resurrection, and thee fellowship of his sufferings, being made conformable unto his death;(Philippians 3:8-10).

Paul welcomed personal suffering as a means of further knowing his Lord.

Beginning in the Millennium years, and continuing into the eternal Heavenly life, the infinite knowledge of Jesus will be available.

> Now unto him that is able to do exceeding abundantly above all that we ask or think, according to the power that worketh in us, Unto him be glory in the church by Christ Jesus throughout all ages, world without end. Amen (Ephesians 3:20-21).

This means that Christ's knowledge will be available to pursue evolving advances in eternity. This would include medical discoveries that would impact the multitudes of mortals, and their posterity, who survived the Tribulation.

MILLENNIUM OF LIMITLESS TRAVEL

Knowledge will be imparted by Christ for distant travel____ including travel throughout God's creation. The scoffing reader might be reminded that in just over 100 years we have seen glamorous vehicles, greater-than-Titanic's, speeding Amtrak's, roaring jets, soaring space rockets and innumerable satellites____ and probably driverless vehicles by the time this book is written.

The advent of mass travel will enable saints everywhere to fulfil Paul's words to "know as they were known." How wonderful are the words of Christ in Matthew 8:10-11!

> When Jesus heard it, he marveled, and said to them that followed, Verily I say unto you, I have not found so great faith, no, not in Israel. And I say unto you, That many shall come from the east and west, and shall sit down with Abraham, and Isaac, and Jacob, in the kingdom of heaven.

The beneficial increase in travel during the Millennium is discussed further in the following section.

MILLENNIIUM OF WORLDWIDE PREACHING

An important event of the Millennium will be the preaching of the "Gospel of the Kingdom" to the multitudes of unbelievers. It will be the last opportunity of grace before the end (of the Millennium), which will be followed by the beginning of Eternity, or the Heavenly life. Jesus spoke of this witnessing during the Olivet Discourse in Matthew 24, verse 14.

> And this gospel of the kingdom shall be preached in
> all the world for a witness unto all nations; and then
> shall the end come.

There should be no confusion about the latter prophetic statement of Christ, in respect that the context of Matthew 24 is about events following the Tribulation.

At this present time the preaching of the gospel to individuals is not allowed in all nations. However, during Christ's Millennial reign the gospel will be openly preached in all nations. Consequently, the prophecies in Daniel 12 will become reality.

> And they that be wise (teachers) shall shine as the
> brightness of the firmament: and they that turn many
> to righteousness as the stars for ever and ever, But
> thou, O Daniel, shut up the words, and seal the book,
> even to the time of the end: many shall run to and
> fro, and knowledge shall be increased Daniel 1:3-4).

We enumerate several key points from the above Scriptures of Daniel 12. The setting will be near the end time (see Matthew 24:14).

1. There will be some teachers (wise ones, Proverbs 11:30) of the Millennium who will be instrumental in leading unbelievers to Christ. These teachers will have a notable brightness about them, a characteristic of their glorified state, and will comingle with unbelieving mortals.
2. Many mortals will become believers.
3. Travel will be extensive and unimpeded.
4. Knowledge will be increased____ which will be knowledge of the Lord Jesus.
5. This preaching will occur near the end time.

Reception to preaching will be more accepted during the Millennium than during the Tribulation, for at least two reasons: (1) Christ will reign on earth during the Millennium, and (2) lessons will have been learned from the celebrated murder of the two preachers of the Tribulation, described in Revelation 11.

MILLENNIUM OF ONE-WORLD LANGUAGE

We would expect that Christ will reinstitute a uniform language, beginning during the Millennium. The record of the Genesis 11 period described actions by the Trinity to confound the single language of that time, because that people thought to build a physical tower called Babel, to reach the heavens.

Christ's knowledge will enable us to know a Heavenly language, unlike any in this life. There will be no interpreters or crowds speaking in tongues. Communications will be unhindered.

Paul was likely exposed to Heaven's language when "caught up into Paradise", hearing words inexpressible (2 Corinthians 12:3-4).

> And I knew such a man, (whether in the body, or out of the body, I cannot tell: God knoweth) How that he was caught up into paradise, and heard unspeakable words, which it is not lawful for a man to utter.

The language of the future life will facilitate the following:

> That many shall come from the east and west, and shall sit down with Abraham, and Isaac, and Jacob, in the kingdom of heaven (Matthew 8:10-11).

MILLENNIUM OF THE PERFECTING OF MUSIC

Another of the joyful advents of the Heavenly life will include the continual learning of music and praise of our Lord. Music and musical instrumentation have never reached a zenith in this life, inasmuch as the new becomes old after a few months or so. Music has always evolved.

In the future life, where thoughts will be uncluttered from worldly influences, music expression will continually enlarge. The Psalmist David seemed to greatly anticipate the enlargement of music expression in the Heavenly life. But, also Isaiah. And also, John, on Patmos. In citing the following Scriptures, we remind the reader that they are prophetic. The words "new song" are underlined for emphasis.

> Praise the LORD with harp: sing unto him with the psaltery and an instrument of ten strings. Sing unto him a **new song**; play skillfully with a loud noise (Psalms 33:3,4).

> Praise ye the LORD. Sing unto the LORD a **new song**, and his praise in the congregation of the saints (Psalms 149:1).

> I am the LORD: that is my name: and my glory will I not give to another, neither my praise to graven images. Behold the former things are come to pass, and new things do I declare: before they spring forth I tell you of them. Sing unto the LORD a **new song**, and his praise from the end of the earth (Isaiah 42:8-10).

> And they sung a **new song**, saying, Thou art worthy to take the book, and to open the seals thereof: for thou wast slain, and hast redeemed us to God by

thyblood out of every kindred, and tongue, and
people, and nation (Revelation 5:9).

And they sing the song of Moses the servant of God,
and the song of the Lamb, saying, Great and marvelous
are thy works, LORD God, Almighty; just and true
are thy ways, thou King of saints (Revelation 15:2).

An inference may be drawn from Revelation 15:2 that the oft
cited new song will be the Song of the Lamb.

Our Lord is referenced in the Revelation Scriptures on 29
occasions as the Lamb, and as LORD on 22 occasions. We might
suspect that the anthem-like Song of the Lamb may be an endless
reminder in the Heavenly life of God's love for sinners. The timeless
adoration of the Song of the Lamb will touch the depths of our love
for his sacrifice at Calvary.

MILLENNIUM OF THE DOMESTICATION
OF THE ANIMAL KINGDOM

Along with the lifting of the Adamic curse during the Millennium,
life will revert to God's initial provision for animals that were in
Eden. The animals were to be herbivorous.

And to every beast of the earth, and to every fowl
of the air, and to every thing that creepeth upon the
earth, wherein there is life, I have given every green
herb for meat: and it was so (Genesis1:30).

While the environment in Eden was perhaps not a blueprint of
the future life, God remarked seven times about the Genesis 1 events
thus,

And God saw that it was good.

The domestication of animals during the Millennium is vividly described in Isaiah 11:6-9.

> The wolf also shall dwell with the lamb, and the leopard shall lie down with the kid; and the calf ad the young lion and the fatling together; and a little child shall lead them. And the cow and the bear shall feed; their young ones shall lie down together: and the lion shall eat straw like the ox. And the suckling child shall play on the hole of the ask, and the weaned child shall put his hand on the cockatrice's den. They shall not hurt nor destroy in all my holy mountain: for the earth shall be full of the knowledge of the LORD, as waters cover the sea.

The frequent reference to children is an indication that the lifting of the curse will begin during the Millennium, when children will be born of survivors of the Tribulation. However, the Heavenly life, after the 1000 years, will include those who are mature in appearance. The thrust of the scriptures in Isaiah 11 is not taken as illustrative of the precariousness of children, but on the domestication of wildlife.

The domestication of animals implies that an abundance of grain will be available. Life during the Millennium will bring to bear those who till the soil, without the disappointment of the Adamic curse. The available knowledge of the Lord will enhance the joy of this activity.

MILLENNIUM OF MEDICAL AND SCIENTIFIC ADVANCES

Beginning with the lifting of the Adamic curse during the Millennium, the personal reign of Christ on earth will signal major benefits of his knowledge.

The glorified saints will minister to the unsaved survivors of the Tribulation, and their posterity. Great medical advances will benefit children of those survivors, and these survivors will live longer. The following verses (Isaiah 65:17-21) tell of those times.

> For, behold, I create new heavens and a new earth: and the former shall not be remembered, nor come into mind. But be ye glad and rejoice for ever in that which I create: for, behold, I create Jerusalem a rejoicing, and her people a joy. And I will rejoice in Jerusalem, and joy in my people: and the voice of weeping shall be no more heard in her, nor the voice of crying. There shall not be more thence an infant of days, nor an old man that hath not filled his days: for the child shall die an hundred years old; but the sinner being an hundred years old shall be accursed. And they shall build houses, and inhabit them; and they shall plant vineyards, and eat the fruit of them.

It is notable from these Scriptures that individuals will not be given beyond 100 years to trust in Jesus for salvation, lest they be accursed. And, because 100 years could be the age of a child, it seems evident that those who are saved during the Millennium will be under 100 years of age.

AFTER THE MILLENNIUM: OUR HEAVENLY LIFE

The closing of the Millennium will transition into an eternal Heavenly life with Christ and his people. All unbelievers, along with Satan, will go to an unending Lake of Fire. The Great White Throne Judgement of God will consign unbelievers to punishments commensurate with their deeds on earth.

I prefer not to describe Heaven as a place, because that might suggest limitations, notwithstanding that Jesus used the word "place" in John 14. The unlived life of Christians will be anywhere that Jesus is. Rather than a place, I think of our "Heavenly life", because we will be enabled to explore God's creation. Christ will never leave us. Metaphorically, the gates of the city of Heaven will always be open (Revelation 21:25), so that the Heavenly life may extend to distant galaxies, everywhere (except the Lake of Fire). Note that Paul wrote of Heavenly places (plural) in Ephesians 2:4-7)

> But as it is written, Eye hath not seen, nor ear heard, neither have entered into the heart of man, the things which God hath prepared for them that love him (1 Corinthians 2:9).

> But God, who is rich in mercy, for his great love wherewith he loved us, Even when we were dead in sins, hath quickened us together with Christ, (by grace ye are saved) And hath raised us up together, and made us sit together in heavenly places in Christ Jesus: That in the ages to come he might shew the exceeding riches of his grace in his kindness toward us through Christ Jesus (Ephesians 2:4-7).

In the above Scriptures Paul informed that (1) God has prepared unimaginable blessings for believers in Christ (2) that, throughout eternity God will be showering us with expressions of his kindness, and these graces will be done because of God's love for those who love His Son.

We make much of Paul's words in Ephesians 2, "that in the ages to come." We do not take these words as meaning a future "one-time" gift of God's kindness____ and thereafter we're on our own. Rather, we believe that God will always (eternally) be giving. He will always have surprises for those who cherish His son. We will never be ahead of God's surprises, or out-guess His love.

THE "NO MORES' OF THE HEAVENLY LIFE

Sometimes it's easier to speak of those negatives which will not be a part of the Heavenly life. Revelation 21 lists some of these.

- No dying
- No tears
- No sorrow
- No night
- Nothing that defiles

Additionally, concerning marriage, Christ was clear in the Synoptic Gospels that earth's marital relationship will end (Matthew 22, Mark 12 and Luke 20). The only marriage in the Heavenly life will be that between Christ and his Church.

Christ stated that saints will be like angels, which has generally been understood to be an anatomy void of sexuality. The consequences of his assertion should not be surprising, because glorification of earthly bodies will render saints with bloodless bodies, like that of our post-resurrected Christ. It should also be put to rest that the Heavenly life will not be a quasi-Garden of Eden existence, in the following respects.

- Satan and his followers will obviously not have entrance, because they will be in the Lake of Fire.
- Eden, with all its wonder, had unheavenly restrictions: (1) the Tree of Knowledge of Good and Evil, and (2) residence within Eden.
- The sanctioned conditions of Genesis 1:28 would not be true of the Heavenly life, because they were already imposed.

Eden had some conditions which will be apparently be evident in the Heavenly life.

- Adam and Eve lived as adults in the Garden of Eden, suggesting that Heaven's saints will be mature in appearance. The earthly relationship between human age and physical appearance will not exist in the Heavenly life. To illustrate, Isaiah 65:17-21 speaks of a child being 100 years old during the Millennium.
- The Tree of Life was in the Garden of Eden, and it will be present in the Heavenly life (Revelation 22:2).

CHILDREN OF LIGHT IN THE HEAVENLY LIFE

Being with Jesus means we will be like him.

> Beloved, now are we the sons of God, and it doeth not yet appear what we shall be: but we know that when he shall appear, we shall be like him; for we shall see him as he is (1 John 3:2).

If we now believe that Jesus is the spiritual light of the world, that his physical light blinded Saul on the Damascus Road, that he will destroy the Antichrist at his coming with the physical brightness of his light, that saints of old saw a great light, that the future New Heaven will have no need of the sun because of his physical light____ then we will also be physical light bearers in the Heavenly life to come.

> While ye have light, believe in the light, that ye may be children of light (John 12:36).

> And there shall be no night there; and they need no candle, neither light of the sun; for the Lord God

giveth them light: and they shall reign for ever and ever (Revelation 22:5).

Genesis 1:3 informs that God called his special light into existence three days before any sunlight.

FROM NOW UNTIL THE RAPTURE

Since 1 Corinthians 15:51 teaches that Christians will not receive glorified bodies until the Rapture, what happens before then, when a Christian departs this life? What kind of body?

Scriptures teach that Christians will enter into the presence of our Lord.

Therefore, we are always confident, knowing that, whist we are at home in the body, we are absent from the Lord (for we walk by faith, not by sight) We are confident, I say, and willing rather to be absent from the body, and to be present with the Lord (2 Corinthians 5:6-8).

Lo, I am with you always, even unto the end of the world (Matthew28:20).

The real meaning of death is separation from God. Yes, Christ was separated from God, in his death at Calvary.

Therefore, Christians never die. How true are the words of the Prophet Habakkuk 1:12!

Art thou not from everlasting, O LORD my God, mine Holy One? We shall not die.

In what kind of body do Christians live when they enter into the Lord's presence? One Scripture stands out, among many:

> For we know that if our earthly house of this
> tabernacle were dissolved, we have a building of God,
> an house not made with hands, eternal in the heavens.
> For in this we groan, earnestly desiring to be clothed
> upon with our house which is from heaven: If so be
> that being clothed we shall not be found naked (2
> Corinthians 5:1-3)

The above Scripture touches the human spirit in a myriad of ways: (1) We "tabernacle" in this life, in the sense of moving here and there in a tent(metaphor), to our final home with Jesus (2) We began as dust, but God imparted into us a living soul; the dust we leave behind (3) we have an eternal building of God awaiting us (4) eternal in the heavens (plural); Jesus gave comfort that he was preparing a place (singular), but the Heavenly life will be everywhere (heavens), except the Lake of Fire (5) Paul raises the specter of not being without some kind of body. Paul raised the concern which many Christians might occasionally ponder____ that we might be, in some sense, "naked" with our Lord until we receive glorified bodies____ that we might tarry until the Rapture in vapor-like spiritual bodies.

To refute this concern, we declare that Christ returned to Heaven (wherever) in a very real and touchable body (Acts 1). As a reader, you are left to consider the likelihood of our Lord, in his visible body, in fellowship with vapor-like bodies.

Furthermore, those "appearances" of Moses and Elijah on the Mount of Transfiguration were not ghostly spirit beings. God dressed them appropriately, albeit in their Old Testament bodies.

> And it came to pass, that the beggar died, and was
> carried by the angels into Abraham's bosom: the rich
> man also died, and was buried; and in hell he lift up
> his eyes, being in torment, and seeth Abraham afar
> off, and Lazarus in his bosom (Luke16:22-23).

Finally, it seems intuitive that, if the rich man in hell had bodily features then, those who enter into the presence of the Lord will also have some form of body, until their glorified body is received at the Rapture.

End Time Judgements by the Holy Spirit

The Holy Spirit is the third person of the Trinity____ God the Father, Jesus the Son, and the Holy Spirit. Indeed, the very existence of the person of the Holy Spirit is generally rejected by all but fundamental Bible believers.

Humanists are not generally receptive to the biblical teaching of 2 Thessalonians 2, that the Holy Spirit presently restrains____ in the sense of keeping world conditions from spiraling into hopelessness.

> And now ye know what witholdeth that he might be revealed in his time. For the mystery of iniquity doth already work, until he be taken out of the way. And then shall that Wicked be revealed, whom the Lord shall consume with the spirit of his mouth, and shall destroy with the brightness of his coming. (2 Thessalonians 2:6-8)

A fundamental teaching of these verses covers several points about Christ, the Anti-Christ, the Holy Spirit, and the end times.

1. That the mystery of iniquity is more meaningfully recognized by the prevalence of lawlessness, which existed in Paul's time,

and that this lawlessness will greatly increase before Christ returns to earth for the Church i.e., Rapture.

2. That lawlessness was an unrecognized condition "under the radar" in times past.

3. That the mystery of lawlessness will be a masculine person who, in a matter of time, will be revealed. This person will be the Anti-Christ.

4. That this Anti-Christ will be destroyed by the brightness of Christ's coming, which harmonizes with Zechariah 14:12, which relates to the final war against Israel, i.e., Armageddon.

5. That the lawlessness attributed to the Anti-Christ is presently restrained by the power and presence of the Holy Spirit.

6. That the Holy Spirit will, at some point in time, be "taken out of the way", after which the Anti-Christ will be revealed to the world at large. It is generally believed that the removal of the Holy Spirit, as a restraining power, will coincide with the Rapture. Lucifer, or Satan, is the Anti-God angel____ giving rise to a person who will be the Anti-Christ.

A prophecy of Ezekiel provides a prophecy and judgement of Satan.

> Thou shalt be a terror, and never shalt thou be any more (Ezekiel 28:19)

JESUS PROPHESIED OF THE JUDGEMENT ROLE OF THE HOLY SPIRIT

> Nevertheless, I tell you the truth: it is expedient for you that I go away: for if I go not away, the Comforter will not come unto you; but if I depart I will send him unto you. And when he is come, he will reprove the world of sin, and of righteousness,

and of judgement: of sin, because they believe not on me; of righteousness because I go unto my Father, and ye see me no more; of judgement, because the prince of this world is judged. (John 16:7-11)

Verse 13 aids our understanding of the above Scripture.

Howbeit when he, the Spirit of truth, is come he will guide you into all truth: for he shall not speak of himself; but whatsoever he shall hear, that shall he speak: and he will shew you things to come.

JESUS PROPHESIED OF END TIMES BY CITING THE TIMES OF THE NOAHIC FLOOD AND JUDGEMENT AT SODOM GOMORAH

In Luke 17, Jesus described two of God's judgements; (1) the judgement in Noah's day which resulted in the world flood, and (2) the judgement at Sodom Gomorrah. Although sin was an underlying cause, the judgments were different from one another in the following respects:

- The flood of Noah's day occurred because every imagination of the heart was continually evil (Genesis 6:5).
- The firestorm at Sodom occurred because of the perversion of that place____ that even Abraham had difficulty pleading for mercy on Sodom.

CONTRASTING REVELATIONS OF
THE TWO JUDGEMENTS

1. Eight souls were saved from the flood, but only three were saved from the firestorm at Sodom; and these resisted removals from Sodom.

2. During the flood, Mrs. Noah was saved but, of the inferno at Sodom, Jesus sharpened the distinction with the words:

Remember Lot's wife (Luke 17:32)

3. For 120 years Noah preached, during a time when God's patience was evident. However, unlike God's patience before the flood, the pleadings of Abraham and the one-night stay of the two angels at Sodom, spoke of the wrath of God.

4. The judgement of the flood was preceded by scoffers and mockers, who were relatively harmless____ condemning only themselves. But the mockers and scoffers at Sodom were not harmless. They were vicious. They wanted to satisfy their perverse sexual cravings on even the angels. Lot, himself, attempted to bargain his daughter to spare the angels. The perversity at Sodom became physical.

And they said, Stand back. And they said again, This one fellow came in to sojourn, and he will needs be a judge: now will we deal worse with thee, than with them. And they pressed sore upon the man, even Lot, and came near to break the door(Genesis 19:9).

POSSIBLE IMPLICATIONS OF THE CONTRAST BETWEEN THE JUDGEMENTS

- Fewer people will believe in Jesus.
- Evil imaginations of the mind will become realities of perversity.
- Apostasy will increase, including within families.
- Mockers and scoffers of moral right will legalize their ways.
- The fulfilment of 2 Thessalonians 2:6-8 will occur.

Complacency

The Lord our God spake unto us in Horeb, saying, Ye have dwelt long enough in this mount (Deuteronomy 1:6).

After forty years of wandering in the wilderness, Moses told the surviving multitude they had lived there long enough. The first generation had died out, because of unbelief. Now, their children were to enter Canaan. Moses would not be making the journey.

The forty years had been miserable, but people often adapt to misery. And misery often leads to complacency, if nothing better is apparent.

Misery, complacency and fear of the unknown hovered about the survivors. Their fears would later dismay Joshua when the twelve spies returned with a report of giants in Canaan.

The new generation, weakened by complacency and fear, could easily recall the "good old days" __ when God had provided quail and manna for their grumbling parents. The children had never learned to do for themselves.

But, no one was present to confess how their grumbling parents had also been complacent toward their earlier days back in Egypt.

And the mixt multitude that was among them fell a
lusting: and the children of Israel wept again, and said,
Who shall give us flesh to eat? We remember the fish,
which we did eat in Egypt freely; the cucumbers, and
the leeks, and the onions, and the garlick (Numbers
11:4-5).

GOD IMPEDES COMPLACENCY

God intervenes in the lives of complacent people. The foremost
work of the Holy Spirit is to convince sinners of their condition, and
to show them Christ's blood-sacrifice for sins on the cross at Calvary.

LIKE AN EAGLE STIRRING THE NEST,
GOD INCITES US TO ACTIVITY

As an eagle stirreth up her nest, fluttereth over her
young, spreadeth abroad her wings, taketh them,
beareth them on her wings, so the LORD alone did
lead him (Deuteronomy 32:11,12).

Imagine the physical composure of the eaglet during its first
trip on mother's wings____ the shrieking sound when first dropped
through the heavens. On and on the repetitions go, until the eaglet
gets its wings.

The metaphor is a reminder that God sometimes allows recurring
challenges until complacencies are amended.

GOD MOVED ON ELIJAH AT THE BROOK CHERITH

The Brook Cherith (1 Kings) had been a God-appointed refuge
from King Ahab. God commanded ravens to bring bread and meat
to Elijah, both morning and afternoon. After a while the brook dried

up (the stirring of the nest described in Deuteronomy 32), and God commanded Elijah to dwell with a widow for sustenance. While in her company Elijah restored her son to life.

Like the wilderness survivors, God moved Elijah from the potential complacency at the Brook Cherith to work a divine purpose in his life.

Some people may never be helped until their complacencies are resolved. It may be a "cop-out" to conclude that others are available to take your place. In my own life I have had to face realities that God's expectations were on me to make certain hospital visits, to teach certain classes, to witness to certain individuals, to officiate certain funerals.

GOD MOVED ON FOUR LEPERS AT THE GATE OF SAMARIA

And there were four leprous men at the entering in of the gate: and they said one to another, Why sit we here until we die? (2 Kings 7:3).

With the city of Samaria under siege, and no place of welcome inside, the four outcasts asked the life-challenging question. Complacency hovered over their miserable existence. Life offered them few choices. Their fears were resolved with the reckoning that the worst outcome was death.

The ancient story of the four leprous men rings true with many applications:

- Some medical surgeries cannot be resolved by lingering at home.
- Some businesses will not endure without changes.
- Some churches will cease to grow unless actions are taken.
- Some careers will end unless actions are redirected.

COMPLACENY DIVIDES SOME PEOPLE BETWEEN
WHAT THEY POSSESS__ AND WHAT THEY DESIRE

The following account illustrates the often-true story that some complacent individuals are possessed by their possessions.

> And behold, one came and said unto him, Good Master, what good thing shall I do, that I may have eternal life? And he (Jesus) said unto him, Why callest thou me good? There is none good but one, that is, God: but if thou wilt enter into life, keep the commandments. He said unto him, Which? Jesus said, Thou shalt do no murder, Thou shalt not commit adultery, Thou shall not steal, Thou shalt not bear false witness, Honour the father and thy mother, and Thou shalt love thy neighbor as thyself. The young man saith unto him, all these have I kept from my youth up: what lack I yet? Jesus said unto him, If thou wilt be perfect, go and sell that thou hast, And give to the poor, and thou shalt have treasure in heaven: and come and follow me. But when the young man heard that saying, he went away sorrowful: for he had great possessions. Then said Jesus unto his disciples, Verily, I say unto you, that a rich man shall hardly enter into the kingdom of heaven (Matthew 19:16-23).

Doubting Believers

And straightway the father of the child cried out,
and said with tears, Lord, I believe; help thou mine
unbelief (Mark 9:24)

Personal faith sometimes becomes fragmented like that of the
child's father. It may sound well to assert convictions about
imaginary challenges, especially before others. But, is it not true,
that when faith is severely tested, there is sometimes a quivering
unspoken doubt?

UNDERSTANDING THE WAIVERING FATHER

And one of the multitude answered and said, Master,
I have brought unto thee my son, which hath a dumb
spirit; and wheresoever he taketh him, he teareth
him: and he foameth, and gnasheth with his teeth,
and pineth away:and I spake to thy disciples that
they should cast him out; and they could not (Mark
9:17-18).

This was the only child of the desperate father, according to Luke 9.
The lad was withering away. Each episode was taking another toll on
the father. There was no one to help, not even the disciples.

And they brought him unto him: and when he saw him, straightway the spirit tare him; and he fell on the ground, and wallowed foaming. And he asked his father, how long was it ago since this came upon him? And he said, Of a child. And oftentimes it hath cast him into the fire, and into the waters, to destroy him: but if thou canst do anything, have compassion on us, and help us (Mark 9:20-22).

The destructive condition had lingered since childhood, possibly for years. At some point the wretched father realized that, in some special way, he also needed help to cope with the unending conflict.

Beaten down, the years had brought no joy to the father. Each day was like the one before. No hope was in sight, unless Jesus could do something____ anything, to help. The father needed help for his son____ and for himself.

WAS ABRAHAM'S SARAH A DOUBTING BELIEVER?

It is suggested that Abraham's wife, Sarah, was also a doubting believer. The account of Genesis 18 may be recalled, of the Lord's foretelling of a child by Sarah.

And the Lord appeared in the plains of Mamre: and he sat in the tent door in the heat of the day; And he life up his eyes and looked, and, lo, three men stood by him: and when he saw them, he ran to meet them from the tent door, and bowed himself toward the ground (verses 1,2), and they said unto him, Where is Sarah thy wife? And he said, Behold, in the tent. And he said, I will return unto thee according to the time of life; and, lo, Sarah thy wife shall have a son. And Sarah heard it in the tent door, which was behind them. Now Abraham and Sarah were old and stricken in age; and it ceased to be with Sarah after the manner of women. Therefore, Sarah laughed within herself, saying, After I am waxed old shall I have pleasure, my lord being old also? And the Lord said unto Abraham, Wherefore did Sarah laugh, Saying I of a surety bear a child, which am old? Is anything too hard for the Lord? At the time appointed I will return unto thee, according to the time of life, and Sarah shall have a son. Then Sarah denied, saying, I laughed not; for she was afraid. And he said, Nay, but thou didst laugh (verses 9-15).

In this instance Sarah's skepticism was a silent laughter. But the angel interpreted it as a doubt.

Is there any difference between Sarah's apparent doubting and that of the father's unbelief, recorded in Mark 9? We should understand that Sarah and Abraham, like the father, had gone for years in a wanton condition. Like the father of Mark 9, Abraham and Sarah's plight was hopeless____ until the Lord intervened.

WAS MOSES A DOUBTING BELIEVER?

In the Book of Numbers, chapter 20, an event is described during which Moses apparently doubted the provision of the Lord. Serious consequences followed. The event occurred during the wilderness journey of those who followed Moses from Egypt____ at a particular time when the multitude complained for lack of water.

And the Lord spake unto Moses, saying, Take the rod, and gather thou the assembly together, thou, and Aaron thy brother, and speak ye unto the rock before their eyes; and it shall give forth his water, and thou

shalt bring forth to them water out of the rock; so thou
shalt give the congregation and their beasts drink.
And Moses took the rod from before the Lord, as he
commanded him. And Moses and Aaron gathered the
congregation together before the rock, and he said
unto them, Hear now, ye rebels; must we fetch water
out of the rock? And Moses lifted up his hand, and
with the rod he smote the rock **twice:** and the water
came out abundantly, and the congregation drank,
and their beast also. And the Lord spake unto Moses
and Aaron, Because ye believed me not, to sanctify
me in the eyes of the children of Israel, therefore ye
shall not bring this congregation into the land which
I have given them (Numbers 20:7-12).

We have underlined the word "twice" in order to bring out a
discrepancy between the Lord's instruction and the actual action of
Moses. More specific instructions are given in Exodus 17:6.

Behold, I stand before thee there upon the rock in
Horeb; and thou shalt smite the rock, and there shall
water come out of it that the people may drink.

God's instruction to Moses was to smite the rock once. We
cannot discern the reason for the extra blow to the rock. Did
Moses not believe God? Did Moses want to somehow add to God's
instructions____ for good measure? Was Moses angry and frustrated
with the people and, like a sullen child, did he impulsively strike the
rock twice? Was the water slow in coming from the rock? We can
only infer that God saw something of the attitude of Moses. We do
not want to trivialize the incident.

WAS ELIJAH A DOUBTING BELIEVER?

In 1 Kings 19, there is the interesting account of the prophet Elijah, threatened by Jezebel, after the prophet called down fire and destroyed the false prophets of Baal.

> And Ahab told Jezebel all that Elijah had done, and withal how he had slain all the prophets with the sword. Then Jezebel sent a messenger unto Elijah, saying, So let the gods do to me, and more also, if I make not thy life as the life of one of them by tomorrow about this time. And when he saw that, he arose, and went for his life, and came to Beersheba, which belongeth to Judah, and left his servant there. But he himself went a day's journey into the wilderness, and came and sat under a juniper tree: and he requested for himself that he might die; and said, It is enough; now, O Lord, take my life; for I am no better than my fathers (1Kings 19:1-4).

Elijah wanted to die. Ironically, he ran for his life. Elijah was stressed and beaten down by the fiery trials.

THE DOUBTING BELIEVERS OF LIFE

How can Christians cope with stresses which can often seem unending____ stresses which can sometimes raise doubt that anything good could happen?

Platitudes abound. Individuals seem to develop their own methods to cope with life's challenges. There are those who advise to hang with whatever works, but that can only deepen the anxieties if wrong practices are followed____ such as alcoholism, binge eating, excessive spending, etc.

Rev. James R. Hawk

I have always found that faithful church attendance helps me in life's conflicts. By church attendance I mean seeking spiritual strength from hearing the preaching of God's Word., growing in the power of prayer life, and surrounding myself with caring people.

Regular study of the Bible is an invaluable source of encouragement during trying times.

The Manger and the Cross

Sometimes the mental images of Bethlehem's manger and Calvary's cross beg for attention. These images provide the following contrasts.

FIRST CONTRAST

At the manger, we see the humility of his birth.

At the cross, we see the humiliation of his death (Acts 8:33).

SECOND CONTRAST

At the manger, swaddling clothes covered his nakedness

At the cross, we see him made shamefully naked.

THIRD CONTRAST

At the manger, we see innocence in birth.

At the cross, we see guilt for all.

FOURTH CONTRAST

At the manger, we see visitation by shepherds.

At Calvary, we see him despised and rejected.

FIFTH CONTRAST

At the manger, he drank of mother's milk.

At the cross, he was given bitter vinegar.

SIXTH CONTRAST

At the manger, angels sang and welcomed his birth.

At the cross. crowds jeered and welcomed his death.

SEVENTH CONTRAST

At the manger, God sent his son in the fulness of time.

At the cross, Jesus said "it is finished".

Romans 8:28

And we know that all things work together for good to them that love God, to them who are the called according to his purpose.

A PROMISE, A CHALLENGE, A COMFORT

This Scripture encompasses at least three areas of life: promises, challenges and comforts.

Romans 8:28 is surely a promise, but explicitly conditional on having a love for God. Those who do not accept this as a promise are encouraged to review their doctrinal beliefs about the veracity of the Bible.

Romans 8:28 may also be a challenge to your faith. It's sometimes easier to worry than to demonstrate faith. For example, when your neighbor has lost his job, is quoting Romans 8:28 not a challenge? Do you easily share this verse with a young couple going through divorce? I attempted to use this verse many years ago on the day when my youngest son's girlfriend left him. Disaster!

Romans 8:28 is a source of great comfort___ after we have waited on the Lord. Life has many examples where we can look back and sigh with comfort about how things worked out. Several examples are listed below.

- I'm glad that I did not marry that other person.
- I'm glad that I acted patiently during that time.
- I'm glad that I had my health exam when I did.

Can you list or recall five "I'm glad's" from your past?

THE IMPORTANCE OF "ALL THINGS"

To those who love the Lord we say, with sometimes trembling voice, it must be ALL things working for good. All things. All things__ future. Not some things.

Consider something which may be bothering you at this present time. Your job? A troubled relationship? A health problem? Whatever. Now, if you do not fully agree with Romans 8:28__that matters will work out for your good__ then you are left to be fearful and to worry. But then, in your fearful and anxious condition, consider the verse from 2 Timothy 1:7.

> For God hath not given us the spirit of fear, but of
> power, and of love, and of a sound mind.

Thus, if you dismiss Romans 8:28, then you are left to something of which God has no part. You have allowed another spirit to influence your life_____ a spirit of fear.

As difficult as it may seem, the events in your life will ultimately serve for good, according to your you love for God. However, you could not have told Moses this when he killed an Egyptian, nor David when he had Uriah slain, nor Peter when he denied his Lord. There are consequences for wrong actions.

However, if you love the Lord, then you will experience his forgiving power, and come to realize his mercy and grace.

DO RANDOM THINGS WORK FOR OUR GOOD?

Some people look for a "sign" in everything. The Bible states that rain comes down on the just and the unjust, that many of the same things happen to all people. We should not expect to be immune from random events which may challenge us, but rather to know that God is in control of our lives.

HOW DOES GOD WORK THINGS TOGETHER FOR GOOD?

While we could never know all the ways of God's workings, we may learn much from Bible teachings, as well as life experiences.

God often works things out for good in the lives of his people over a period of time, and through circumstances. Time and circumstances go together.

However, the importance of time and circumstances in the outworking of Romans 8:28 is not as simple as assuming that outcomes will be as we anticipate. Patient waiting on God to act in our best interest oftentimes reveals that God's provision is far better than what we had originally set our sights on. For example, I'm now glad that my college romance with another girl fell apart, although I was hurt at that time

Patiently waiting on the Lord, through time and circumstances, generally results in a better outcome. Conversely, there are those who make snap decisions (courtship, marriage, career, etc.), and want God to clean up their mess afterwards. The latter statement may not be inspiring to the reader who has already gone from one crisis to another. God's abilities are not in question, but rather our learning and grasp of God's will. Thus, it is said of the prodigal son, recorded in the gospels,

When he came to himself...

Many people of the Bible found goodness, after the manner of the prodigal son, Jonah, Peter, Samson, and David__ to mention a few.

Sometimes God works things out for good in his people who, without apparent fault, endure suffering over a period of time. The rise of Joseph to prominence in Egypt comes to mind. Thus, God may be preparing some individuals for special callings, only after they have endured trials.

Lastly, we must realize that many dear souls experience continual suffering in this life. We have mental images of their beds of suffering, their pitiful condition, their loneliness. And often times caretakers carry heavy burdens. How can you, being aware of Romans 8:28, provide encouragement to these poor souls? The answer seems to be in a nearby verse, Romans 8:18:

> For I reckon that the sufferings of this present time
> are not worthy to be compared with the glory that
> shall be revealed in us.

ALL THINGS WORK TOGETHER FOR GOOD--OUR GOOD, OR GOD'S?

Are you anticipating how things will turn out right for you____ or right with God? You may want a promotion in the workplace, but God may want you gone to a better job. Sometimes we must be brought to the place of learning that our ways are not God's ways.

The application of Romans 8:28 may be missed if our priorities are misplaced.

TO THEM THAT LOVE GOD, TO THEM
WHO ARE "THE" CALLED

Romans 8:28 is specifically God's provision for those who love him. Indeed, Romans 8:28 is not for called people, but "the" called. God's people are set apart (1 Peter 2:9).

Despite God's condition on Romans 8:28, there are those who abuse and confuse its meaning. Trite and untrue encouragements abound, which are sometimes spoken to unsaved people during their misfortune. We hear these false encouragements frequently. Some are listed below.

- Better days lie ahead.
- When the going gets tough, the tough get going.
- Keep your head up.
- Your loved one has a new guitar (or whatever) in Heaven; he/she is looking down now.
- Your friend is driving a new race car in Heaven.
- He/she is a role model.

What is your response upon hearing a remark such as one above? Should you respond? Why?

Morning Glories No. 3

The Lord hath given me the tongue of the learned, that
I should know how to speak a word in season to him
that is weary: he wakeneth morning by morning, he
wakeneth mine ear to hear as the learned. Isaiah 50:4

We have named these Heavenly blessings morning glories.
They are gifts from our Heavenly father, like manna in the
wilderness of the biblical exodus. May these gifts be mental and
spiritual nourishments, as our encampment moves closer to our
Heavenly home.

This meditation is much about being an encourager. The task is
more difficult for some than others.

Pitiful complaints sometimes abound of inability to speak to
others___ excuses of not being properly schooled, or that someone
else is better suited. Like Moses of old, many need an Aaron.

But, lest we elevate our importance, the scripture states that it
is our Lord who awakens and enables us to be an encouragement to
others.

However, there may be a plausible excuse for silence on some
occasions, because God instructs us to "speak a word in season."

Some spoken words may be "out of season" on some occasions. Is the scripture advising that the words be limited?

Hopefully, most everyone has some notion to steer away from improper speeches during times that are inappropriate. Few people may want to hear Romans 8:28 during the heat of a crisis.

But if the ministry of encouragement is to be successful, there may also be something better than words____ no matter how sincerely the words are expressed. Kind actions are perhaps always welcome.

I have told grieving folk that I am praying for them, and I received token smiles. But my wife baked a nice cake for many, and warm hugs of appreciation were evident. Many times, I have done my best at funerals to help people know the God of all comfort. But many times, the simple act of visiting a family, a few days later (in season), seemed to provide more meaningful encouragement.

Appropriate words and actions provide encouragement to others, when done in season.

However, our best encouragement may simply be that of being present for others who may be searching for direction. Listeners may sometimes be great encouragers.

This meditation is about the Lord bringing weary people to our minds, more than words which we may express. Weary people are all about us____ relatives, work associates, church members, friends at school, neighbors, shoppers in the market place____ hurting people are everywhere.

The most encouraging person may be the one most friendly, who cares not if he or she is speaking to a relative, or a stranger. There are weary lonely individuals in the food market who may allow you into their world if you allow then to precede you at checkout.

I am just now reminded how that several years ago we began inviting a lonely widow into our home on special occasions to share with our children. We delighted in giving her extra food to take home. Fun photographs were made. She was always given a Christmas gift. Upon her death, she surprised our family with a wonderful gift of money.

Morning Glories No. 4

What is man, that thou shouldst magnify him? And that thou shouldst set thy heart upon him? And that thou should visit him every morning, and try him every moment? (Job 7:17-18)

In his despair of life, Job acknowledged the important truth of the existence of a personal God, with caring attributes.

Those attributes apply between God and all mortals, not merely Job, i.e. "what is man". In speaking for all mortals, the patriarch asserted that God magnifies his highest creation__ declaring that God visits every morning.

God's great love for every person is expressed elsewhere, in 2 Peter 3:9:

> (...) not willing that any should perish, but that all should come to repentance.

You are unable to comprehend the depths of God's love for you. A consequence is that he looks in on you every day (morning). Is this a larger picture of a loving parent looking in on a sleeping child?

It is something awesome to think about, but God's love for you is new every day.

> It is of the Lord's mercies that we are not consumed, because his compassions fail not. They are new every morning: great is thy faithfulness (Lamentations 3:22-23).

In visiting you every morning, with new compassions, God lingers by you____ moment by moment. You are never left alone. You may think at times that you are possibly running from God, but he is always near. You are tested____ not daily or weekly____ but every moment.

God's time provision for you is measured in moments. He is not into hours, weeks or earth time. Notice the underlining of "moment in the following verses.

> Knowest thou not this of old, since man was placed upon earth, that the triumphing of the wicked is short, and the joy of the hypocrite but for a **moment**. (Job 20: 4,5)

> Therefore, hear now this, thou that are given to pleasures, that dwellest carelessly, that sayest in thine heart, I am, and none else beside me; I shall not sit as a widow, neither shall I know the loss of children: But these two things shall come to thee in a **moment**, in one day, the loss of children and widowhood: (Isaiah 47:8,9)

> Behold I show you a mystery: We shall not all sleep, but we shall all be changed, in a **moment**, in the twinkling of an eye, at the last trump; for

the trumpet shall sound, and the dead shall be raised incorruptible, And we shall be changed. (1 Corinthians 15:51,52)

The lifespan of the penitent thief at Calvary trickled down to a few moments before a life-changing decision was made.

The time lapse between this life and the next is but a moment.

Morning Glories No. 5

The burden of Dumah. He calleth to me out of Seir, Watchman, what of the night? Watchman, what of the night? The watchman said, The morning cometh, and also the night: if ye will enquire, enquire ye: return, come (Isaiah 21:11-12).

The original meaning of the short oracle seems lost in antiquity. I prefer to think that God's prophet was being asked how much longer unrighteousness would abound (what of the night?). This supposition is made because of the line of questioning and the answers.

This negative inquiry invited a negative response. Surprisingly, the unexpected reply was positive, that the morning (light) was coming. While there could be many interpretations, the most comforting thought is that of the return of Christ.

However, God also completely responded to the initial question____ that the night was also coming. Could this speak of the final judgement of the unbeliever?

The negative question "what of the night?" reflects a current society which often callouses people into a negative mindset, whereby nothing good is anticipated.

How often do Christians face discouraging events day after day! How do we find relief from negative and hurtful outlooks in the daily grind?

We might look at one of God's prophets, Jeremiah. He became so discouraged by surroundings that he dreamed of a "shady rest" motel in the wilderness.

> Oh that I had in the wilderness a lodging place of wayfaring men; that I might leave my people, and go from them! For they be all adulterers, an assembly of treacherous men (Jeremiah 9:2).

Another uplifting perspective is found in the writings of Habakkuk. The prophet saw wickedness all about himself.

> Why doest thou shew me iniquity, and cause me to behold grievance? For spoiling and violence are before me: and there are that raise up strife and contention. Therefore, the law s slacked, and judgement doth never go forth: for the wicked doth compass about the righteous; therefore, wrong judgement proceedeth (Habakkuk 1:3-4).

However, against this dreary outlook, Habakkuk proclaimed a very positive outlook for God's people.

> Art thou not from everlasting, O LORD my God, mine Holy One? We shall not die (Habakkuk 1:12).

To every report of troubling news, you are encouraged to keep the following words close to your memory.

> The morning cometh

This is more than a quick catch-phrase. It opens the door of eternal hope of every Christian, which hope is cited in the following verse.

> I Jesus have sent mine angel to testify unto you these things in the churches. I am the root and the offspring of David, and the bright and morning star (Revelation 22:16).

The Language Of Tears

For out of much affliction and anguish of heart I
wrote unto you with many tears (2 Corinthians 2:4).

Some emotions are inexpressible. They lie deep within the spirit__
can only be stirred by tears. Can there be hidden tears, ready to
spill outwards__ if not subdued?

WHY DID JESUS WEEP AT THE TOMB OF LAZARUS?

What emotions prompted the tears of Jesus? Because a loving
family had become separated? Because the master of death had gazed
on Lazarus? Because sin in the human race was once more apparent?
Because Jesus foresaw himself separated from God, at Calvary?
Because he struggled with his humanity? Because he was setting set
an example for all mankind, that it was okay to weep?

Who can discern the language of tears?

What is the depth of meaning of a mother's tears, when told her
child is no more? Who can tell the fakery of a forced smile? What
is written in the tears of a child, so unprepared for hurt and shame
and shattered dreams. Will the child grow old and never tell of the
sorrows of innocent years?

JESUS' FEET WERE WASHED WITH TEARS

> And, behold, a woman in the city, which was a sinner,
> when she knew that Jesus sat at meat in the Pharisee's
> house, brought an alabaster box of ointment, and
> stood at his feet behind him weeping, and began to
> wash his feet with tears, and did wipe them with the
> hairs of her head, and kissed his feet, and anointed
> him with ointment (Luke 17:37-38).

We are caught starring into this mental picture of a lonely outcast honoring God's Son. Could Heavenly hosts have gazed on this spectacle? She spoke no words. But Christ, who looks on the inside, read the language of her tears.

How powerful was the language of her tears? For she was a sinner, she had done no worthy deeds, she was an outcast, she spoke no words. Yet, by her humble and speechless actions, she gained Heaven.

> Wherefore I say unto thee, Her sins, which are many,
> are forgiven; for she loved much: but to whom little
> is forgiven, the same loveth little. And he said unto
> her, Thy sins are forgiven (Luke 7:47-48).

WHY DID JESUS CRY OUT AT CALVARY?

What emotions were included in the language of his tears? What expressions measured the wrath of God at Calvary? What words heaved the weight of all ninth- hour sins? From the language of the Hebrew writer, what was meant by "strong crying"?

GOD IS MOVED BY TEARS

Weary of running from King Saul, young David seemed to recognize that his tears moved God.

Thou tellest my wanderings: put thou my tears into thy bottle: are they not in thy book (Psalms 56:8)?

Labors for the Lord have promise of joy and victory, when bathed in tears.

> They that sow in tears shall reap in joy. He that goeth forth and weepeth, bearing precious seed, shall doubtless come again with rejoicing, bringing his sheaves with him (Psalms 126:5,6).

There is the familiar account of King Hezekiah's tears, recorded in 2 Kings, chapter 20, in which the Prophet Isaiah brought sad news that the king faced death____ and those tears moved God.

> In those days was Hezekiah sick unto death. And the prophet Isaiah the son of Amoz came unto him, and said unto him, Thus saith the Lord, Set thine house in order; for thou shalt die, and not live. Then he turned his face to the wall, and prayed unto the Lord, saying, I beseech thee, O Lord, remember now how have walked before thee in truth and with a perfect heart, and have done that which is good in thy sight. And Hezekiah wept sore. And it came to pass, afore Isaiah was gone out into the middle court, that the word of the Lord came to him saying, Turn again and tell Hezekiah the captain of my people; Thus saith the Lord, the God of David thy father, I have heard thy prayer, I have seen thy tears: behold I will heal thee:

on the third day thou shalt do into the house of the
Lord. And will add unto thy days fifteen years;

We are left to meditate on two aspects of Hezekiah's prayer; (1)
his testimony of himself, and (2) his tears.

THE ENDING OF THE LANGUAGE OF TEARS

And God shall wipe away all tears from their eyes; and
there shall be no more death, neither sorrow, nor crying,
neither shall there be any more pain, for the former things
are passed away. (Revelation 21:4)

Realizing the finality of tears opens for us a wider view of
Heaven. On earth, tears are a language of hidden secrets. Some
sorrows we have never learned to express. We had never really
gotten over many heartaches__ even with the blessed help of God's
Comforter. We just tried to put on our best face while on earth. Our
secret hidden tears were not far away.

With the ending of tears in Heaven, there will be no sorrowful
secrets that will hinder our eternal joys.

Baca

Blessed is the man whose strength is in thee; in whose heart are the ways of them. Who passing through the valley of Baca make it a well (Psalms 84:5-6).

This Psalm is attention-getting, in identifying special blessings to those of exceptional Godliness.

In every age there have been exceptional people of God, however imperfect, who were unusually blessed. Indeed, the future rewards of Heaven support the existence of people who excelled in running their race well.

One distinctive feature of these exceptional people is their "passing through" a valley identified as Baca.

The little word, Baca, means place of sorrow, tears, anxiety. Baca need not be so much a geographical place, as an experience in the life of every individual.

Figuratively, Baca is an experience of all mortals. Baca impacts all people____ in prison houses, troubled homes, drug crowds, abortion clinics, cemeteries, career setbacks, closed factories, divorce courts; for these are places of sorrow, tears and anxiety. We may say that men, women and youth go down to Baca each day____ often not aware of the sorrows of journey's end.

You, as a reader of this meditation, may be on the outskirts of Baca just now____ sensing anxiety in your life. The question is, how long will you tarry in Baca before passing through? On the other hand, you may have vivid memories of having passed by that troubling experience.

Our Lord passed by way of Baca during his earthly sojourn. Amidst the joys of earthly fellowship, he was not home in glory with the Father. Calvary was the very heart of our Lord's journey through Baca. His utterance on the cross, "it is finished", signaled the end of his humiliation.

The Bible includes the sad plight of many who ventured to Baca.

- Did not Jonah board an ill-fated ship to Baca?
- Where did rebellious Samson die, if not in Baca?
- Did not Abraham lie about his relationship with Sarah down in Baca?
- Where is the grave of King David's sinfully conceived baby, if not near Baca?
- Are not the graves of Mahlon and Chilion, and their father Elimelech, located in Baca__ far from Bethlehem? Perhaps never revisited by Naomi.
- After the first night in Sodom Gomorrah, did Lot not realize that he had taken his family to a Baca-like place?
- Did not the Prodigal Son leave the comforts of home for the far country of Baca?
- When Peter denied his Lord was there not a sudden impulse that he was warming by the fires of Baca's citizenry?

While every child of God experiences the sorrow of Baca at times in life, it is exhilarating that Psalms 84:6 states "passing through" to describe God's grace.

Not only do the children of God pass through Baca, but Psalms 84:7 gives encouragement that they grow stronger in the seasons of life, i.e., "they go from strength to strength." This experience of growth is the beginning of exceptionality.

Furthermore, Psalms 84:11 indicates that God will not withhold good things from his blessed children.

How do God's people rise to an exceptional level of blessedness? Although many profess salvation, why do we see some who appear exceptionally blessed more than others?

The condition of exceptional blessing should not be confused with having inordinate material possessions. For example, some may be materially poor in this world but incredibly rich in spirit and faith towards God. Exceptional blessings may also include having Godly children, grandchildren or a wonderful spouse, or many years of a Godly marriage, or rich friendships.

For example, I feel blessed in having exceptional Godly parents who brought me up in the local church____ which literally began with community prayer meetings in two or three homes, one of which was ours. I recall neighbors crowding into our home for the evening service. Their first clapboard formal church is being razed at this writing, to be replaced with a multimillion dollar sanctuary. However, my parents never attended high school, and were much closer to being materially poor than otherwise

The only lasting wealth is a rich relationship with God, as related by Jesus in Luke 12:20-21:

> But God said unto him, Thou fool, this night thy souls shall be required of thee: then whose shall those things be, which thou hast provided? So is he that layeth us treasures for himself, and is not rich toward God.

Psalms 84 describes the lifestyles of Godly people who are especially blessed.

First, exceptionally-blessed people are those who love the Church.

This love is alluded to in the opening verse, and beautifully stated in verse 10:

> I had rather be a doorkeeper in the house of my God,
> than to dwell in the tents of wickedness.

Secondly, Psalms 84:2 describes exceptional Godly people who have a hungering for the things of God. The following verse informs of a spiritual (soul) attraction, complimented with a physical (flesh) attraction.

> My soul longeth, yea, even fainteth for the courts of
> the Lord: my heart and my flesh crieth out for the
> living God.

Thirdly, Psalms 84:4 highlights God's blessed ones who pass through Baca__ they are settlers in God's house. Settlers are often those who give praise to God.

Fourthly, Psalms 84:3 teaches that God's blessed ones are those who rear their children in Church life, while they are very young.

Fifthly, Psalms 84:5 teaches that the blessed man recognizes that his strength comes from God.

The Psalmist emphasizes the theme of blessedness with his closing verse:

> Blessed is the man that trusteth in thee.

Can there be Any Good Thing Come out of Nazareth?

John 1:43-51

THE COMPANION FRIEND

Some of the disciples had discovered Jesus, the Messiah, and quickly shared the good news with friends. Peter found Nathaniel, who replied "can any good thing come out of Nazareth?"

We cannot say that Nathaniel's reply was a push-back. Christians can sometimes be cynical. But friends should tell friends about Jesus. It seems ironical, if not hypocritical, that some Christians seem more willing to witness to strangers about Jesus, than the very ones with whom they are close.

You may live hundreds of miles from family and friends, and you may have difficulty witnessing to loved ones. However, your calls, written messages and gifts may prove to have great value. It seems sad that some families seldom get together until the passing of a loved one.

THE COMPLAINT

Nathaniel's question may come across as being cynical. Christians have long become accustomed to veiled mockery.

In every area of life there seems to be those negative people who question most everything. Some are bitter and hurt about something. You may be quite "green" in witnessing for Jesus if you have never confronted some of these.

Christian witnessing is neither arguing with another, nor displaying superior Bible knowledge. Sometimes the best verbal witnessing is sharing the simple truth about what Jesus has done in your life.

THE CONVICTION: COME AND SEE

Philip's response to Nathaniel's question was one of invitation and personal conviction, "come and see."

Jesus used these same three words on the previous day to invite two disciples to his dwelling place.

There are many occurrences of the simple invitation "come" in the Bible. They are gentle, unimposing invitations, which seek change, but are followed by blessings. A few examples are provided.

> Come now, and let us reason together, saith the Lord: though your sins be as scarlet, they shall be as white as snow: though they be red like crimson, they shall be as wool (Isaiah 1:18).

> Come unto me, all ye that labor and are heavy laden, and I will give your rest (Matthew 11:28).

> And the Spirit and the bride say, Come. And let him that heareth say, Come. And let him that is athirst come. And whosoever will, let him take of the water of life freely (Revelation 22:17).

THE CHOOSING

The question of who saw the other first, Jesus or Nathaniel, is important, as noted in verses 47-48.

> Jesus saw Nathaniel coming to him, and saith of him, Behold an Israelite indeed, in whom is no guile! Nathaniel saith unto him Whence knowest thou me? Jesus answered and said unto him, Before that Philip called thee, when thou was under the fig tree, I saw thee.

Clearly, Jesus saw Nathaniel first. It may not be obvious to you, but Jesus saw you before you were born. His desire is toward you.

The subject of the meditation is "Can there be any good come out of Nazareth?" This question has been affirmatively answered millions of times__ and need not be revisited.

The more timely question is "what good things can come from your life?"

I love the Lord, because...

Psalms 116

How wonderful, that God has provided you written reasons for loving him, notwithstanding that you likely have some good reasons of your own.

The chapter overwhelms with its beginning words, raising expectations of blessed encouragements to follow.

HE LISTENS (VERSES 1-2)

> I love the Lord, because he hath heard my voice and my supplications. Because he hath inclined his ear unto me, therefore will I call upon him as long as I live.

Just think, the King of Heaven has time for you. Our age of idle waiting, taking numbers, and listening to background music on the phone does not apply. You have direct personal contact through the Holy Spirit. It is our Lord's present role as High Priest to listen to believers. However, if you do not speak then you will not be heard.

What a blessed opportunity you have__ "as long as I live." Surely, you have come to read one of our Lord's reasons for loving him.

HE LIFTS (VERSE 6)

The Lord preserveth the simple: I was brought low,
and he helped me.

Your salvation has elevated you to a position which the world may not understand. Your hope is in Christ, not the sordid and often depressing generation about you.

Our Lord desires that you love him, because you have been lifted from the dredges of a complicated and sinful life to simple faith in the finished work of Christ at Calvary.

HE LEADS (VERSE 8)

For thou hast delivered my soul from death, mine eyes
from tears, and my feet from falling.

Your salvation has a rationale of listening, lifting and leading that leads to victorious living. When you became one of the sheep of his pasture, the Great Shepherd became the caretaker of your life.

You should make much of the emphasis of the spiritual over the physical, noting the soul is mentioned before the flesh. Conversely, professing love for the Lord on the basis of physical blessings alone, without regard to spiritual health, is hollow idolatry.

HE LOADS WITH BENEFITS (VERSE 7 AND PSALMS 68:19)

Return unto thy rest, O my soul: for the Lord hath
dealt bountifully with thee. (verse 7)

> Blessed be the Lord, who daily loadeth us with
> benefits, even the God of our salvation, Selah.
> (Psalms 68:19).

This meditation has surely brought you to a place of utter inability to grasp all the benefits of your salvation___ peace, joy in the Lord, grace, forgiveness of sin, faith, presence of the Holy Spirit, hope, assurance, comfort___ is there any end to God's bountiful blessings?

You should not leave the above verses without pondering these thoughts: (1) you have spiritual (soul) rest in the provision of God's benefits (2) you are "loaded" with benefits__ not burdens, but innumerable blessings, and (3) you are equipped and blessed each day.

HE FREES FROM BONDS (VERSES 16)

> O Lord, truly I am thy servant; I am thy servant, and
> the son of thy handmaid; thou hast loosed my bonds.

Bondage of some form is a way of life in this world. Some forms of bondage, such as that of holy matrimony, are to be valued.

However, there are other wrongful forms of bondage from which you can be free, in Christ. Because your salvation has elevated you to __"greater is he that is in you than he that is in the world"(1 John 4:4)__ the burden of fear and sins is removed.

> Come unto me all ye that labor and are heavy laden,
> and I will give you rest.

> For God hath not given you the spirit of fear, but of
> power and love and sound mind.

Encouragements from Habakkuk

WE SHALL NOT DIE (Habakkuk 1:12)

What an incredible encouragement! At a time when danger abounded, God informed the prophet that there would be no dying of the saints. A list of some of the turmoil of the times is listed below, with chapter and verse.

- Violence (1:2)
- Strife (1:3)
- Plundering (1:3)
- Legal injustice (1:4)
- Wickedness ((1:13)
- Addictions (1:15)
- Idolatry (1:16)
- Pride (2:5)
- Alcoholism (2:5)
- Homebreaking (2:5)
- Coveting (2:5)

The list of sins is too much like that of our day to arouse our senses, beyond "what's new?".

Those words, "We shall not die", could just as easily have come from Moses, marching across the bed of the Dead Sea ____ or from Daniel's three Hebrew children, dancing in the fire.

The four little words from Habakkuk are the "amen and the hallelujah" to the question of old that was asked by the Patriarch Job.

If a man die, shall he live again? (Job 14:14)

Those words are now anchored in the spirit and soul of all whose trust is in Jesus Christ.

Habakkuk heralded the true meaning of death: eternal separation from God. He affirmed that God's children will not be separated from God. Paul's words ring more clearly,

> We are confident, I say, and willing rather to be absent from the body, and to be present with the Lord (2 Corinthians 5:8)

Jesus made Habakkuk's watch cry all the more hopeful:

> And whosoever liveth and believeth in me shall never die (John 11:26).

I WILL STAND UPON MY WATCH, AND SET ME UPON THE TOWER (Habakkuk 2:1)

The Old Testament reference to tower, whether literal or not, represented a condition of watchfulness.

Jesus encouraged watchfulness throughout the gospels, and also in Revelation 3:2 and 16:15. The calls for watchfulness are generally focused on watching for the coming of the Lord.

There is blessed continuity between Habakkuk's assertion that we will not die, and his resolve to be watchful. If God's people are assured of eternal life, then joyful anticipation of the Lord's return seems quite natural.

However, Habakkuk's encouragements are also valuable for our daily Christian walk. The following encouragement speaks to our lifestyle before Christ comes.

THE JUST SHALL LIVE BY HIS FAITH (Habakkuk 2:4)

What strange words come from so far into the past! Where did the old prophet find these words__ so opposite the Commandments? It's almost like divine excitement during the Old Covenant, anticipating a blessed walk of faith.

It's amusing, and fanciful, to think that Habakkuk penned these words, corked them into a bottle__ and that bottle washed up at Paul's feet (Romans 1:17)

Euroclydon

But not long after there arose against it a tempestuous wind, called Euroclydon (Acts 27:14).

And when neither sun nor stars in many days appeared, and no small tempest lay on us, all hope that we should be saved was then taken away (Acts 27:20).

All hope taken away! How did conditions deteriorate so badly? It's a universal question for many.

- How did the once hopeful marriage fade?
- How did school grades suddenly decline?
- How did all the resources become wasted?
- What happened to health?
- How did freedom detour into bondage?
- When did the experiment become a habit?
- Where are my friends?

All hope taken away____ how? This indicting question raised frowning faces in Bible times.

- Blind Samson could have asked himself how conditions sank so low.
- Naomi may have sobbed over the question at family graves in distant Moab.
- The question dogged Lot while stumbling from the inferno at Sodom.
- The impoverished prodigal son pondered the losses.
- King David moaned over the question__ more than once. No hope! Where is Absalom?
- How could all hope disappear? _____ an eternal question for Judas Iscariot.

THE EUROCLYDON DRAMA AT SEA

It was a real-life drama____ acted out on a ship carrying the prisoner Paul to Rome. The 276 souls onboard included a wealthy merchant, slaves, prisoners, sailors, a courteous Roman centurion named Julius, and the ship's captain.

Fierce cyclonic winds blew up in the Mediterranean during the late fall voyage, as winter approached. These tempestuous northeasterly winds were called Euraquilo in the Revised Version. Here (KJV), in Acts 27, the wind was called Euroclydon.

The ship-board drama began near the isle of Crete, where the winds picked up, and Paul warned against further sailing at that time. His warning was ignored. From Crete the ship was on a course to hopelessness.

"I-TOLD YOU-SO": REMINDERS FROM PAUL

At the height of the storm Paul stood in the midst and remarked (Acts 27:21),

Sirs, ye should have hearkened unto me, and not have loosed from Crete, and to have gained this harm and loss.

Who are we to question Paul? We do not question, but simply observe that "I-told-you-so" reminders are generally not well received.

Neither do not diminish the importance of Paul's initial warning at Crete, but, alas, initial warnings are often ignored. Oh, that many initial warnings were heeded.

- the first speeding citation
- the first parental admonition
- the meteorologist's initial hurricane brief
- the minister's first invitation to salvation,
- the physician's initial advice.

ARE WE NOT ALL ON A VOYAGE?

Is not everyone set on a course in some direction____ in marriage, in career path, in health management, in retirement____ in issues of life? Are we not time-travelers? As with Paul's voyage, are we not thrown together with diverse people, having varied interests? And do not life-storms threaten us along our journeys?

LIKE PAUL, OUR FATE IS OFTEN CHALLENGED BY A FEW PEOPLE

After Paul's warning not to leave Crete, we note the following rejection in verse 11,

> Nevertheless, the centurion believed the master (captain) and the owner of the ship, more than those things which were spoken by Paul.

Like Paul, we are not always free to pick and choose acquaintances. Diversity abounds, with varying demands and circumstances

Like Paul, those people in our circle may have contrary views____ and potential problems can be significant. A student's career path may be altered by one difficult professor. One troubled member of the family may disrupt harmony. Only one misguided supervisor may result in lasting problems.

However, God's word is replete with examples where his followers stood by holy convictions____ and were later honored. Some Old Testament examples were Moses, Joshua, Habakkuk, Daniel, Elijah and Elisha, Mordecai.

While it is true that we are not always free to choose our surroundings, we should learn from those occasions where wrong choices were made. Examples include Lot at Sodom, and Peter, warming by the fires, while Christ was under arrest.

LIKE PAUL, WE MAY BE CONFRONTED BY A MAJORITY

As the intensity of the storm increased an apparent vote was taken.

> And because the haven was not commodious (suitable)
> to winter in, the more part advised to depart thence
> also, if by any means they might attain to Phenice,
> and there to winter (Acts 27:12).

Authority was initially restricted to the master and owner of the ship (verse 11), but here, as the storm progressed, the restricted authority gave way to shared authority. The "more part" became advisers. Understandably, this number probably did not include the larger population of slaves and prisoners onboard.

Weak leaders who face pushback often resort to shared authority, projecting a self-preserving democratic posture. The interrogation of

Jesus by Pilate, Herod and religious leaders is one example. Notice the chain of events, beginning in Luke 23:1.

> And the whole multitude of them arose, and led him(Jesus) unto Pilate.

Then, notice the apparent shirking or "easy out" by Pilate in verse 6.

> And as soon as he (Pilate) knew that he (Jesus) belonged to Herod's jurisdiction, he sent him to Herod,

Then, note the back-and-forth completed by Herod in verse 11.

> And Herod with his men of war set him (Jesus) at nought, and mocked him, and arrayed him in a gorgeous robe, and sent him again to Pilate.

Finally, note Pilate's further sharing of authority with the religious leaders, in Matthew27:22.

> Pilate saith unto them, what shall I do then with Jesus which is called Christ?

The climactic surrender of Pilate is noted in Matthew 27:24.

> When Pilate saw that he could prevail nothing, but that rather a tumult was made, he took water, and wash his hands before the multitude, saying, I am innocent of the blood of this just person: see ye to it.

Christians may often be "out-voted" in important issues of life. For example, some laws of the land may challenge faith, against clear Bible convictions. Such convictions arise from study of God's Word and prayer for wisdom, as promised in chapter one of the Book of James.

The faithful stance of God's people in making decisions may be illustrated by the example of Joshua,

> (...) as for me and my house, we will serve the Lord (Joshua 24:15).

LIKE PAUL, WE WITNESS THE EFFECT OF LIFE'S STORMS ON PRIORITIES

The peak of the storm brought desperation, imminent danger, and a decision to lighten the load in the ship.

> And we being exceedingly tossed with the tempest, the next day they lightened the ship; and the third day we cast out with our hands the tackling of the ship (Acts:27:18-19).

Some may cling to material treasures until imminent death hovers about. Idol trinkets may have been accumulated, which will not be easily turned loose. Only near the final hour might there be divesture of those little false goodies____ causing dissension among jealous loved ones____ or adding more burden to the local landfill.

Can you hear the loud sales pitch of distant kinfolk at a garage sale __ hawking those leftover treasures? "Take both of these for only seven dollars, and the dishes will be thrown in extra. These shoes were hardly worn__ take them for five dollars."

Death, like Euroclydon, has a way of changing ownerships.

> Yea, I hated all my labour which I had taken under the sun: because I should leave it unto the man that shall be after me. And who knoweth whether he shall be a wise man or a fool? (Ecclesiastes 2:18-19).

The Patriarch Job and His Children

Job 1

We cannot conclude that Job was a model father from available Scripture, which describes events when his children were grown.

The ancient book is not about the children, but rather Job__ and his struggles with Satan. The limited information of chapter 1 attests to the Godly nature of Job. However, the spiritual nature of his children is guesswork.

UNITY EXISTED AMONG JOB'S CHILDREN

> And his sons went and feasted in their houses, every
> one his day; and sent and called for their three sisters
> to eat and drink with them (Job1:14).

We might conclude that Job instilled unity in his family. It seems clear that he treated each of the children with respect, so that no basis for jealousy existed.

The scripture suggests that the sisters were treated with respect by the brothers. The siblings lived in separate houses, which might imply they were successful.

We cannot assume that the children possessed any of the Godliness of their father. For all that we know, they may have been spoiled by Job's wealth, or they may not have been on speaking terms with him, or they may have had disdain for hanging around the homeplace, or they may have lived their lives like the prodigal son, i.e., as in a far country. It's painful to think in this manner, but such is sometimes true of life.

JOB'S DAY BEGAN WITH CONCERN
FOR HIS CHILDREN

> And it was so, when the days of their feasting were gone about, that Job sent and sanctified them, and rose up early in the morning, and offered burnt offerings according to the number of them all: for Job said, It may be that my sons have sinned, and cursed God in their hearts. Thus did Job continually (Job 15).

The last sentence suggests that Job's day began with spiritual concern for his children. There is no mention of any favorites.

Job's priestly role for each of his children is a humbling example for Godly fathers. Each child may not have been mindful of any personal sin____ but Job acted as the "daysman" (Job 9:33) between each child and God.

JOB'S CARE FOR HIS CHILDREN HINTS
OF CHRIST'S INTERCESSION

The priestly role of Job was a faint foreshadowing of Christs' mediation for believers. In both priestly roles we observe continual and unconditional love for each of the family, emphasizing the importance of absolution of sin.

Inasmuch as the children were likely unaware of Job's priestly intercession each morning, it's more unlikely that we will ever know of the full extent of Christs' priestly passions for us.

A Desire to Be with Christ, "Which is Far Better" ___ Paul's Views

> For I am in a strait betwixt two, having a desire
> to depart, and be with Christ; which is far better
> (Philippians 1:23).

Desires and decisions are generally accompanied by reasons. There are usual reasons for job changes, relationship decisions, and destination choices. But here, Paul does not elaborate. However, in other Scriptures Paul provides reasons for life in Heaven with Jesus.

We may speculate about Paul's yearnings to be with Jesus, without fully knowing the major influences. Hopefully, our speculations will draw us closer to Paul's earthly shadow, enabling us to personally share from his joy for Heaven.

PAUL REASONED THAT EARTH'S SUFFERINGS WERE SMALL COMPARED TO HEAVEN'S GLORY

> For I reckon (reason, conclude) that the sufferings of
> this present time are not worthy to be compared to
> the glory which shall be revealed in us (Romans 8:18).

Some of Paul's sufferings are described in 2 Corinthians 11:24-27.

His desire to be with the Lord was in realization of a far better life in Heaven.

Is there any hint that Paul's desire to be with Christ was motivated by an attitude to be free of his earthly "thorn in the flesh" (2 Corinthians 12)? No such motive seems evident.

Whatever the nature of Paul's affliction, he asked the Lord three times to remove it. We cannot minimize the severity of the malady, and it may have progressively worsened. However, rather than becoming a habitual complainer, Paul took on a positive attitude.

> Most gladly therefore will I rather glory in my infirmities, that the power of Christ may be upon me. Therefore, I take pleasure in infirmities, in reproaches, in necessities, in persecutions, in distresses for Christ's sake: for when I Am weak, then am I strong. (2 Corinthians 12:9-10).

Earlier in the same letter (2 Corinthians 4:17) Paul downplayed his earthly affliction.

> For our light affliction, which is but for a moment, worketh for us a far more exceeding and eternal weight of glory.

Paul desired to be with Jesus, irrespective of any earthly sufferings. His positive attitude seems to contrast with that of many suffering saints, who may sometimes appear more interested in the future life as a haven of escaping the afflictions of this life.

PAUL'S DESIRE TO BE WITH THE LORD WAS BASED ON REVEALED KNOWLEDGE OF HEAVEN

In Romans 12 Paul described an encounter with Christ fourteen years earlier during which he was "caught up to the third heaven."

Paul's revelation of Heaven was apparently spiritual, according to 1 Corinthians 2:9-10.

> But as it is written, Eye hath not seen, nor ear heard, neither have entered into the heart of man, the things which God hath prepared for them that love him. But God hath revealed them unto us by his Spirit: for the Spirit searcheth all things, yea the deep things of God.

We do not know the details of Paul's Heavenly encounter. But we may speculate that even the most meager glimpse of the future life would inspire his desire to depart and be with the Lord.

PAUL'S DESIRE TO BE WITH THE LORD WAS BASED ON A MONUMENTAL TRANSFORMATION IN HIS LIFE

Our Lord's transforming power changed everything about Paul's life.

> For our conversation (citizenship) is in heaven; from whence also we look for the Saviour the Lord Jesus Christ; Who shall change our vile body, that it may be fashioned like unto his glorious body, according to the working whereby he is able to subdue all things unto himself (Philippians 3:20,21).

The transformation that began on the Damascus Road evolved into a bond of intimacy, as suggested in Philippians 3:10.

> That I may know him, and the power of his
> resurrection, and the fellowship of his sufferings,
> being made conformable unto his death.

Do your sufferings bring you into a purposeful fellowship with Jesus? What would this fellowship include? Prayers? Tears? Thankfulness? Bible study? Thoughts of Jesus? Thoughts of the future life? Contrition? Repentance? Other?

PAUL'S DESIRE TO BE WITH THE LORD WAS AN ADMISSION OF AN INFERIOR EARTHLY STATUS

> But what things were gain to me, those I counted
> (Paul's reasoning) loss for Christ. Yea doubtless, and
> I count all things but loss for the excellency of the
> knowledge of Christ Jesus my Lord: for whom I have
> suffered the loss of all things, and do count them but
> dung, that I may win Christ. (Philippians 3:7-8).

Paul's use of the word "reckon" in Romans 8:18, and threefold usage of "count" should not suggest a casual choice, but instead, careful reasoning.

PAUL'S DESIRE TO BE WITH THE LORD RECOGNIZED THE END OF AN EARTHLY RACE, FOLLOWED BY A HEAVENLY REIGN

Nearing the end of his earthly life, Paul penned these words, recorded in 2 Timothy 4:6-8.

> For I am now ready to be offered, and the time of my
> departure is at hand. I have fought a good fight, I have
> finished my course, I have kept the faith: Henceforth there

is laid up for me a crown of righteousness, which the Lord,
the righteous judge, shall give me at that day: and not to
me only, but unto all them also that love his appearing.

It may be informative to note the King James wording of "depart"
in Philippians 1:23, and "departure" here in 2 Timothy. The Greek
transliteration is *luo,* meaning "to loosen".

The same Greek word, transliterated *luo*, was used years earlier
by Jesus in ordering the graveclothes of once-dead Lazarus to be
removed, i.e., "Loose him, and let him go" (John 11:44).

Clearly, Paul viewed his earthly departure as a loosening, or
release, from bonds which had kept him from being with his Lord.

PAUL'S DESIRE TO BE WITH THE LORD
HIGHLIGHTED HIS PASSION FOR THE CHURCH

Paul's letter to the Church at Corinth identified himself with the
saints that would be "caught up" to be with the Lord in the air. Paul
anticipated the rapturous change during his lifetime.

Behold, I show you a mystery; We shall not all sleep
(die), but we shall be changed, in a moment, in the
twinkling of an eye, at the last trump: for the trumpet
shall sound, and the dead shall be raised incorruptible,
and we shall be changed (1 Corinthians 15:51-52).

Before his salvation on the Damascus Road, Paul persecuted
the churches. Afterwards, he ministered to them. Looking into the
future, Paul saw the perfection of the church in a metaphorical bridal
role with his Lord.

That he might present it to himself a glorious church,
not having spot or wrinkle, or any such thing; but

that it should be holy and without blemish. (Ephesians 5:27).

PAUL'S DESIRE TO BE WITH CHRIST WAS A GLIMPSE OF PERPETUITY

That in the ages to come he might show us the exceeding riches of his grace in his kindness toward us through Christ Jesus. (Ephesians 2:7)

The time span___ "that in the ages to come" ____ informs us that God will continually surprise us with good things___ with exceeding riches.

But as it is written, Eye hath not seen, nor ear heard, neither have entered into the heart of man, the things which God hath prepared for them that love him. But God hath revealed them unto us by his Spirit: for the Spirit searcheth all things, yea the deep things of God (1 Corinthians 2:9-10).

We quickly dispel the notion that Heaven is a lazy-like place where saints idly stroll about. Neither should we think of a man and his wife living together, in a mansion, or otherwise, with a common mailbox out front. Get over it.

Heaven will never become uneventful. God has revealed this by his Spirit. Consider, for example, when you were very young that you knew of nothing called a television___ only a radio (I am thinking of older readers). Now, with the passage of little time, you have those flat screens on several walls___ displaying actions of people___ all in color__ in high definition. A "DVR" might have been considered a disease in the 1940s. Change is a meaningful part of our DNA.

If you allow yourself to think of the Heavenly life as an unchanging place, then you may be like the employee in the U.S. Patent office who quit his job in the early 1900s__ walked away, complained that everything had already been invented.

Opportunistic Christian Witnessing

Cast thy bread upon the waters: for thou shalt find it after many days. Give a portion to seven, and also to eight, for thou knowest not what evil shall be upon the earth. If the clouds be full of rain, they empty themselves upon the earth: and if the tree fall toward the south, or toward the north, in the place where the tree falleth, there it shall be. He that observeth the wind shall not sow; and he that regardeth the clouds shall not reap (Ecclesiastes 11:1-4).

An inspiration for this Scripture may be related to the sowing of seed along the river bottoms in Egypt before flood tide____ enabling an interim harvest period.

A SOWER WENT OUT TO SOW

The Scripture highlighted the potential gains of an opportunity. The fertile land adjacent to receded water presented a window of opportunity. The seeds were to be indiscriminately sown, as opposed to the more structured and time- consuming method of planting by spaces in rows.

Opportunistic Christian witnessing means sharing Christ with others, as opportunities emerge.

- Sharing Christ with another in a grocery line
- Sharing Christ at an appropriate encounter in the hardware store
- Sharing Christ during a timely encounter with a neighbor, or new neighbor
- Sharing Christ through a card or E-mail
- Sharing Christ to a handyman
- Sharing Christ during an appropriate encounter with someone in the workplace
- Sharing Christ with someone at a sports event
- Sharing Christ during a hospital visit

Opportunistic witnessing means being brief, but effective. Smiles help. Forget about going to someone's home and getting an hour of their time. No big Bible. No salvation pamphlets. Get around to saying what Christ means to you. Speak briefly and effectively of your church. Avoid the car salesman fervor. God did not call you to be a beggar__ just a sower. Opportunistic witnessing means "a word (not a sermon) in season", from "the tongue of the learned."

> The Lord hath given me the tongue of the learned, that I should know how to speak a word in season to him that is weary: he wakeneth morning by morning, he wakeneth mine ear to hear as the learned (Isaiah 50:4).

Opportunistic witnessing is not suggested as a replacement for launching trainees at midweek from your church. However, those formal witnessing groups may experience shortcomings if they simply meet at the church for thirty minutes of pie and cake, followed by visiting a missing saint who has an ingrown toe nail. If structured witnessing efforts fail to producing tangible results (professions of salvation, growth in classes) then changes are in order.

STRUCTURED VERSUS OPPORTUNISTIC WITNESSING

During my first week as pastor in a large city, I was driven by a church leader to visit prospects in the community. Without exception, I was taken to upscale neighborhoods. Very few residents opened their doors.

Structured Christian witnessing that targets only certain people may not be God-blessed. The parables of Matthew 13 teach that seed was sown on all manner of soils.

A memorable example of opportunistic Christian witnessing occurred during my pastorate of a few years ago. I was witnessing in a neighborhood with a layman, but no one on my list was home. About to call it quits for the day, I was attracted to an older mobile home sitting off on a hillside.

A few knocks on the door brought a man, I suppose in his sixties, who cautiously welcomed us. As he partially opened the door, I informed him that I was a minister in the community, and asked if a brief visit would be okay. Such trembling in a human body I had never before witnessed! Moved by his condition, I stated that we would return at another time, if our presence made him feel uncomfortable.

The trembling man quietly gestured for us to enter. He sat on a small metal half-bed, but its vibration again prompted me to state that we would return later if we made him feel uncomfortable.

That afternoon the trembling man professed faith in Jesus Christ. During the following weeks and months, he quietly entered and left the services from where I pastored.

A few years later, after I had left that pastorate, I was attracted to a very crude casket while in a nearby funeral home. I could not resist approaching the simple unadorned plywood box. I will always cherish my privilege of witnessing to that dear trembling man.

SOMETIME SOWERS

Give a portion to seven, and also to eight,

The above portion of our Scripture instructs that Christian witnessing begins by first putting somethings behind. The number eight signifies a new beginning, i.e., there were eight souls on Noah's ark. The number seven signifies completeness. I am partial to my way of summarizing the above verse____ close one chapter of your life and start a new one.

However, this is unrealistic to many. Consider the "chapter-change" in the life of the farmer, Elisha.

> So he (Elijah) departed thence, and found Elisha the son of Shaphat, who was plowing with twelve yoke of oxen before him, and he with the twelfth: and Elijah passed by him, and cast his mantle upon him. And he left the oxen, and ran after Elijah, and said, Let me, I pray thee, kiss my father and my mother, and then I will follow thee. And he said unto him, Go back again: for what have I done to thee? And he (Elisha) returned back from him, and took a yoke of oxen, and slew them, and boiled their flesh with instruments of the oxen, and gave unto the people, and they did eat. Then he arose, and went after Elijah, and ministered unto him (2 Kings 19:19-21).

There are not many Elisha's in the world, who sever all material relationships to serve Christ. There are relatively few dedicated people like my friends Joe and Linda, who quit good jobs, locked their doors and went away for twenty years on a church planting mission.

As an alternative, dedicated Christians should search within themselves for inspiration to witness for Christ in an opportunistic manner. Balancing life's priorities makes opportunistic witnessing all the more practical.

The goal of every dedicated Christian should be to become a steady sower of God's message to unbelievers__ not a sometime sower.

STORM-WATCHING SOWERS

> If the clouds be full of rain, they empty themselves
> upon the earth: and if the tree fall toward the south,
> or toward the north, in the place where the tree
> falleth, there it shall be. He that observeth the wind
> shall not sow; and he that regardeth the clouds shall
> not reap (from Ecclesiastes 11).

You have no control over a rainy day, and not much more over the direction of a falling tree. During the early years of my ministry, my Christian witnessing was sometimes hindered by people who wanted to talk more about the weather than spiritual life.

I am not at total loss in dealing with the rain-worshippers. A partial solution evolved when, during my sermons, the rains fell heavily onto the church roof__ and attentions shifted to the downpour. I learned to pause briefly from my sermon, and loudly quote the following verse:

> Nevertheless, he left not himself without witness,
> in that he did good, and gave us rain from heaven,
> and fruitful seasons, filling our hearts with food and
> gladness (Acts 14:17).

STRUCTURED SOWERS

Cast thy bread upon the waters

The instruction speaks of indiscriminate sowing. Applying this metaphor to Christian witnessing, the following verse teaches that we are to be ready always to witness for Christ with any person. However, there is a prerequisite of spiritual readiness on our part.

> But sanctify the LORD God in your hearts: and be ready always to give an answer to every man that asketh you a reason of the hope that is in you with meekness and fear (1 Peter 3:15).

Another wonderful verse which calls ministers to readiness is from 2 Timothy 4:2.

> Preach the word; be instant in season, out of season…

A problem sometimes arises when Christian servants bring so much structure into their efforts that the work of the Holy Spirt is hindered.

Reflecting on my own mistakes, I think it is possible to try too hard in Christian witnessing, and also in sermon delivery___ to the extent that the work of the Holy Spirit may be hindered. The following incident of the first year of my ministry speaks of my obsession with excessive sermon notes.

My sermon notes were ridiculously excessive that first year. My homiletics were awful. I was afraid that I might forget to include something important in my sermon____ or go blank altogether.

My dependence on excessive notes was significantly reduced when invited to speak at a country church, located high in the mountains. Many of the congregants grew and harvested Christmas trees for American markets; others leased their land for such. The hillsides surrounding the quaint little church were covered with the beautiful trees.

After I was introduced, I approached the lectern, and opened my Bible, exposing my abundant sermon notes. All too late, I realized that those hard- working folk open the windows to their sanctuary, to allow the heavenly breezes from the fragrant Christmas trees. My numerous notes blew all around. A lengthy prayer was made, but I was not able to gather all materials. Enough said. I feel somewhat embarrassed just recalling that incident.

DISTANT HARVESTS

> Cast thy bread upon the waters: for thou shalt find it
> after many days.

Jeff had made a profession of faith in Jesus Christ, but in less than two years he was back on drugs, and worldlier than ever.

I was both disheartened and confused. His initial response to my Christian witnessing had seemed so genuine. His faithful church attendance, his baptism, his witnessing to others, his praying at the altar____ had I missed something? He had written and published a slick brochure of what Christ had done in his life. His wife and little girl were in church with him. His grandmother was thrilled. Some in the community were amazed that someone so wildly destructive could have been tamed.

But Jeff's old lifestyle returned, sometime about a year after I left the pastorate. Their marriage quickly ended. Jeff wasted years of his life in and out of the local jail. Because of his intimidating size he ruled the cellblock. My friend, an officer in the jail, informed me that tv programs in the cellblock were first approved by Jeff. Sometimes the breakfast of others became his.

In and out of jail, Jeff's drug habits and rough lifestyle eventually landed him in a distant prison. My friend at the local jail told me that I did not want anything to do with Jeff. I learned that gangs of inmates at the distant prison were not the least intimidated by Jeff's burly appearance.

Twenty-five years passed, and Jeff became a distant memory.

However, in 2015, I received a call from the local funeral home to officiate Jeff's funeral. I consented, but soon wondered why I had made myself available for the service. What could I possibly say about Jeff? Where had this wild man been for twenty-five years?

With dreary face, I joined the procession line to view the deceased at the funeral home. What a terrible sight! The once-gentle giant was unsightly, with numerous tattoo's covering his face, including his eyelids. I wished to be somewhere else. Anywhere.

Minutes before Jeff's funeral service, the director of the funeral chapel approached me____ stating that two older ladies desired to talk with me. The lades had made a special trip from one-hundred miles away to tell me about Jeff's life of the last few years.

Jeff had located in that distant large city, and he had lived next door to their church. The ladies informed me that Jeff was very faithful in attendance____ that on Wednesday evenings he taught special classes, which included helping those with a dependency on drugs.

Perhaps there was something in common between Jeff and Samson of biblical times (Judges 16). I've grown fonder of the verse "Cast thy bread upon the waters: for thou shalt find it after many days."

About the Author

The author pastored several churches during a thirty-five-year period, before his retirement in 2016. He published *They Came from Germany, Aboard the Thistle* a historical account of German migration to America. His formal education included the University of Tennessee, Knoxville and Graham Bible College. He taught for two years at Northeast State Community College in East Tennessee.

The author and his wife, Darlene, of fifty-four years have three sons and five grandchildren.

Printed in the United States
By Bookmasters